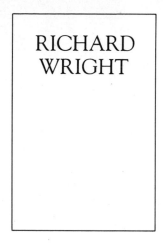

RICHARD
WRIGHT

RICHARD WRIGHT

❧

Joan Urban

Senior Consulting Editor
Nathan Irvin Huggins
Director
W.E.B. Du Bois Institute for Afro-American Research
Harvard University

New York   Philadelphia

Chelsea House Publishers

Editor-in-Chief   Nancy Toff
Executive Editor   Remmel T. Nunn
Managing Editor   Karyn Gullen Browne
Copy Chief   Juliann Barbato
Picture Editor   Adrian G. Allen
Art Director   Maria Epes
Manufacturing Manager   Gerald Levine

Black Americans of Achievement

Senior Editor   Richard Rennert

Staff for RICHARD WRIGHT

Associate Editor   Perry King
Copy Editor   Brian Sookram
Deputy Copy Chief   Ellen Scordato
Editorial Assistant   Jennifer Trachtenberg
Picture Researcher   Andrea Reithmayr
Assistant Art Director   Lorraine Machlin
Designer   Ghila Krajzman
Production Coordinator   Joseph Romano
Cover Illustration   Daniel Mark Duffy

First Printing

1   3   5   7   9   8   6   4   2

Library of Congress Cataloging-in-Publication Data

Urban, Joan F., 1950–
   Richard Wright / Joan F. Urban.
      p.   cm.—(Black Americans of achievement)
   Bibliography: p.
   Includes index.
   Summary: Traces the life and achievements of the Black American novelist.
   ISBN 1-55546-618-4
         0-7910-0254-3 (pbk.)
   1. Wright, Richard, 1908–1960—Biography—Juvenile literature.
2. Authors, American—20th century—Biography—Juvenile literature.
3. Afro-American—Intellectual life—Juvenile literature.
[1. Wright, Richard, 1908–1960.   2. Authors, American.   3. Afro-Americans—Biography.]   I. Title.   II. Series.   88-34614
PS3545.R815Z85 1989   CIP
813'.52—dc 19   AC

Grateful acknowledgment is made to John Hawkins and Associates, Inc., for permission to reprint portions of the following poems by Richard Wright: "I Have Seen Black Hands," copyright © 1934 by Richard Wright, originally printed in *New Masses 10;* and "Red Leaves of Red Books," copyright © 1935 by Richard Wright, originally printed in *New Masses 5.*

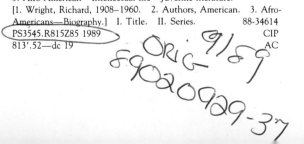

CONTENTS

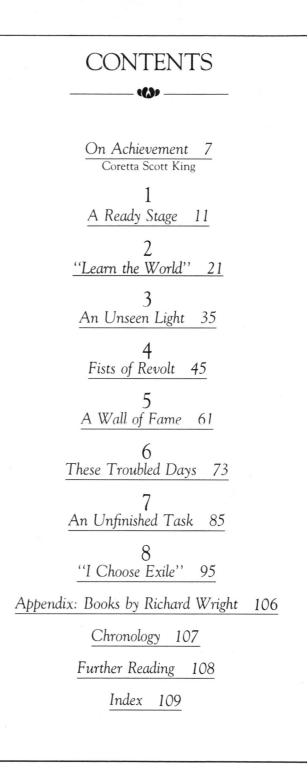

BLACK
AMERICANS
OF
ACHIEVEMENT

—— ✦ ——

MUHAMMAD ALI
heavyweight champion

RICHARD ALLEN
*founder of the
African Methodist
Episcopal church*

LOUIS ARMSTRONG
musician

JAMES BALDWIN
author

BENJAMIN BANNEKER
*scientist and
mathematician*

MARY McLEOD BETHUNE
educator

BLANCHE K. BRUCE
politician

RALPH BUNCHE
diplomat

GEORGE WASHINGTON CARVER
botanist

CHARLES WADDELL CHESTNUTT
author

PAUL CUFFE
abolitionist

FREDERICK DOUGLASS
abolitionist editor

CHARLES R. DREW
physician

W. E. B. DuBOIS
educator and author

PAUL LAURENCE DUNBAR
poet

DUKE ELLINGTON
bandleader and composer

RALPH ELLISON
author

ELLA FITZGERALD
singer

MARCUS GARVEY
black-nationalist leader

PRINCE HALL
social reformer

WILLIAM HASTIE
educator and politician

MATTHEW HENSON
explorer

CHESTER HIMES
author

BILLIE HOLIDAY
singer

JOHN HOPE
educator

LENA HORNE
entertainer

LANGSTON HUGHES
poet

JAMES WELDON JOHNSON
author

SCOTT JOPLIN
composer

MARTIN LUTHER KING, JR.
civil rights leader

JOE LOUIS
heavyweight champion

MALCOLM X
militant black leader

THURGOOD MARSHALL
Supreme Court justice

ELIJAH MUHAMMAD
religious leader

JESSE OWENS
champion athlete

GORDON PARKS
photographer

SIDNEY POITIER
actor

ADAM CLAYTON POWELL, JR.
political leader

A. PHILIP RANDOLPH
labor leader

PAUL ROBESON
singer and actor

JACKIE ROBINSON
baseball great

JOHN RUSSWURM
publisher

SOJOURNER TRUTH
antislavery activist

HARRIET TUBMAN
antislavery activist

NAT TURNER
slave revolt leader

DENMARK VESEY
slave revolt leader

MADAME C. J. WALKER
entrepreneur

BOOKER T. WASHINGTON
educator

WALTER WHITE
political activist

RICHARD WRIGHT
author

ON
ACHIEVEMENT

Coretta Scott King

BEFORE YOU BEGIN this book, I hope you will ask yourself what the word excellence means to you. I think that it's a question we should all ask, and keep asking as we grow older and change. Because the truest answer to it should never change. When you think of excellence, perhaps you think of success at work; or of becoming wealthy; or meeting the right person, getting married, and having a good family life.

Those important goals are worth striving for, but there is a better way to look at excellence. As Martin Luther King, Jr., said in one of his last sermons, "I want you to be first in love. I want you to be first in moral excellence. I want you to be first in generosity. If you want to be important, wonderful. If you want to be great, wonderful. But recognize that he who is greatest among you shall be your servant."

My husband, Martin Luther King, Jr., knew that the true meaning of achievement is service. When I met him, in 1952, he was already ordained as a Baptist preacher and was working towards a doctoral degree at Boston University. I was studying at the New England Conservatory and dreamed of accomplishments in music. We married a year later, and after I graduated the following year we moved to Montgomery, Alabama. We didn't know it then, but our notions of achievement were about to undergo a dramatic change.

You may have read or heard about what happened next. What began with the boycott of a local bus line grew into a national movement, and by the time he was assassinated in 1968 my husband had fashioned a black movement powerful enough to shatter forever the practice of racial segregation. What you may not have read about is where he got his method for resisting injustice without compromising his religious beliefs.

He adopted the strategy of nonviolence from a man of a different race, who lived in a distant country, and even practiced a different religion. The man was Mahatma Gandhi, the great leader of India, who devoted his life to serving humanity in the spirit of love and nonviolence. It was in these principles that Martin discovered his method for social reform. More than anything else, those two principles were the key to his achievements.

This book is about black Americans who served society through the excellence of their achievements. It forms a part of the rich history of black men and women in America—a history of stunning accomplishments in every field of human endeavor, from literature and art to science, industry, education, diplomacy, athletics, jurisprudence, even polar exploration.

Not all of the people in this history had the same ideals, but I think you will find something that all of them have in common. Like Martin Luther King, Jr., they all decided to become "drum majors" and serve humanity. In that principle—whether it was expressed in books, inventions, or song—they found something outside themselves to use as a goal and a guide. Something that showed them a way to serve others, instead of living only for themselves.

Reading the stories of these courageous men and women not only helps us discover the principles that we will use to guide our own lives but also teaches us about our black heritage and about America itself. It is crucial for us to know the heroes and heroines of our history and to realize that the price we paid in our struggle for equality in America was dear. But we must also understand that we have gotten as far as we have partly because America's democratic system and ideals made it possible.

We are still struggling with racism and prejudice. But the great men and women in this series are a tribute to the spirit of our democratic ideals and the system in which they have flourished. And that makes their stories special and worth knowing. ❧

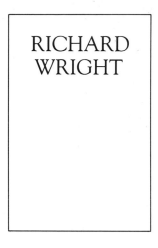

RICHARD
WRIGHT

ST. JAMES THEATRE

NESCA REALTY CO., INC.

THE · PLAYBILL · PUBLISHED · BY · THE · NEW · YORK · THEATRE · PROGRAM · CORPORATION

Beginning Sunday, May 11, 1941 • Matinees Saturday and Sunday

ORSON WELLES and JOHN HOUSEMAN
in association with Bern Bernard
present

A MERCURY PRODUCTION

NATIVE SON

by

PAUL GREEN and RICHARD WRIGHT

(From Mr. Wright's novel of the same name)

PRODUCTION by ORSON WELLES

Settings by James Morcom

with

Canada Lee	Ray Collins	Everett Sloane	Erskine Sanford
Paul Stewart	Anne Burr	Evelyn Ellis	Philip Bourneuf

CAST

(In order of their appearance)

BIGGER THOMAS .... CANADA LEE

HANNAH THOMAS .... EVELYN ELLIS

VERA THOMAS .... HELEN MARTIN

1
A READY STAGE

ON THE EVENING of March 24, 1941, a tense, expectant silence fills the St. James Theatre in New York City. A capacity crowd sits in the darkened playhouse and waits for the curtain to go up on what promises to be an exciting new drama by author Richard Wright. Based on his recently published novel, *Native Son*, it is one of the first works by a black writer ever to be performed on a Broadway stage.

Wright, a slight man who has never quite made up for his childhood years of impoverishment and near starvation, is sitting in the audience. He perches nervously on the edge of his cushioned seat and every now and then rubs his two moist palms together. Known to the world as a poet, short-story writer, novelist, and political activist, at the age of 32 he is about to make his debut as a playwright. He reaches over to Ellen, his wife of just two weeks, and grasps her hand to calm his opening night jitters.

Wright knows that *Native Son* does not present a comforting view of the world. The play, like all his writings, offers a realistic portrayal of how harsh life is for blacks in America. For too long, writers (black as well as white) have kept a filmy gauze over reality and have avoided dealing directly with the topic of race. *Native Son* is different. Instead of depicting blacks as happy-go-lucky—a characterization to which theater audiences have long been accustomed—it focuses on the full horrors of racial discrimination.

Wright's own stage adaptation of his best-selling first novel, Native Son, *opened in 1941 at the St. James Theatre in New York City. Like the book, which had been published one year earlier and established Wright as the first black writer to gain a large mainstream audience, the play offered an uncompromising look at black ghetto life.*

11

The main character of *Native Son* is Bigger Thomas, an angry and demoralized black youth from an urban ghetto. He is barely educated, and his prospects for the future look bleak. Although he dreams of leading a better life, he knows his dreams will most likely go unfulfilled.

Bigger blames most of his hardships on white society, which will not admit blacks into its privileged world. "They don't let us do nothing," he says of whites. "Every time I think about it I feel like somebody's poking a red-hot iron down my throat. Goddamn it, look! We live here and they live there. We black and they white. They got things and we ain't. They do things and we can't." Full of fear and hatred for whites, he is a mass of teeming frustration bound to erupt into violence at any moment.

IN MARCH 1940, when the book version of *Native Son* first appeared in print, the public was ready to take notice of Bigger's plight. "Few other recent novels have been preceded by more advance critical acclamation, or lived up to the expectations they aroused so well," the *New York Times* reported on the morning that the book was published. Wright's strikingly honest depiction of black life strongly affected readers of all races, and he became one of America's best-known novelists practically overnight.

Several months later, Wright sought to reach an even larger audience by bringing *Native Son* to the stage. To accomplish this, he had to transform the book's many pages of text into action and dialogue. He called on Paul Green, an experienced playwright, to help him with the adaptation. Green had written the highly acclaimed *In Abraham's Bosom*, which had won the Pulitzer Prize for Drama in 1927. He was also the author of *Hymn to the Rising Sun*, which was, in Wright's estimation, the most realistic play about blacks ever written by a white dramatist.

In July 1940, shortly after Green agreed to take on the project, Wright hurried to Chapel Hill, North Carolina, to visit Green at his home and begin their collaboration. Wright was anxious to complete the play while the novel was still receiving a great amount of press. The two men sat side by side on Green's expansive porch and worked feverishly into the long summer nights. Eventually, they honed the novel into 10 dramatic episodes.

Both Wright and Green knew the success of the play rested in part on finding the right actor to play the role of Bigger Thomas. The Lafayette Theatre in New York's black uptown district of Harlem was the obvious place to look: The city's leading black actors had been gracing the stage of the Lafayette ever since the theater opened in 1913. Paul Robeson and Frederick O'Neal were among the playhouse's best-known

The Lafayette Theatre was the first theater in New York to house a serious black drama company: the Lafayette Players, established by the noted actor Charles Gilpin in 1916. Before then, the city's black entertainers only performed comedy acts and vaudeville routines.

Thirty-four-year-old Canada Lee (shown here) played the role of Bigger Thomas in the original Broadway production of Native Son. *The play's producer, John Houseman, and director, Orson Welles, had previously cast the New York–born actor as Banquo in the Mercury Players' 1936 landmark presentation of* Macbeth.

contemporary performers. But Wright preferred Canada Lee to either of them.

A talented young actor who had previously been a musician and a prizefighter, Lee seemed destined to make a perfect Bigger Thomas. For one thing, he looked the part: His days in the boxing ring had left him with a broken nose and a cauliflower ear. Lee had also grown up in the same sort of urban setting as that of the play, which takes place in Chicago. Lee knew the character inside out. His ability to express Bigger's feelings of frustration and inner rage with a great deal of sympathy won Wright's profound respect, and the two men established what became a lifelong friendship.

Whereas Wright was elated that the right man had been found to play Bigger, Lee was grateful for the role that solidified his reputation as a serious actor. He was also pleased at the chance to bring a meaningful portrayal of black life to the stage. As he later told reporters for *Negro Digest*, "We're making history in the theater. The Negro has never been given the scope that I'm given in this play. . . . Now they'll think of the Negro as an actor and not as some butler-valet type, some ignorant person."

Wright's faith in Lee's ability to portray Bigger Thomas was seconded by producer John Houseman and the noted actor and filmmaker Orson Welles, who was serving as the director of *Native Son*. With their 1936 production of William Shakespeare's *Macbeth* at the Lafayette Theatre, Houseman and Welles had already staged one of the most notable black productions the drama world had ever seen. They were hoping that their latest collaboration would be equally successful.

"I had set my heart on directing this one myself," Houseman said of *Native Son*. "But I was anxious to end my theatrical association with Welles on a note of triumph and I felt that with the strong text of

Wright's book to support him, his direction of *Native
Son* would be more dramatic than mine." A large,
darkly handsome man whom Wright liked to refer to
as "the human locomotive," the 26-year-old Welles
had already established himself as an imaginative
thinker with boundless creative energy. In addition
to his innovative theater work, his first film, *Citizen
Kane*, had just been released to brilliant reviews and
was on its way to being recognized as a motion picture
masterpiece.

Yet Welles, like Wright, had his doubts about
the production of *Native Son*. Much to his dismay,
the script had passed through numerous revisions. In
fact, Green had become so upset with some of
Wright's most recent changes in the script that the
prize-winning playwright had walked out of the theater during the first preview and refused to have anything more to do with the show. He believed that
Wright's version would not hold up to the scrutiny
of the critics.

The production faced another potential hazard as
well: The staging was especially complicated. *Native
Son* featured 10 different sets of various sizes, and the
35 stagehands barely had enough room to move one
set past another.

And then there were the public protests. The final
preview had been picketed by the National Urban
League, an equal opportunity agency for minorities,
with the claim that *Native Son* cast blacks in an un-
favorable light. The Communist party had also picketed the St. James Theatre because Wright, a party
member, had not written the story of Bigger Thomas
according to party guidelines.

But as it turned out, on the night of March 24,
1941, not a single thing went wrong.

*Director Orson Welles (right) ad-
vises a young actor how to pull
his hat over his ears during a re-
hearsal of* Native Son. *A man of
many talents—he was also a
noted actor, producer, and filmmaker—Welles began work on
Wright's play in February 1941,
right after releasing his first motion picture, the now-classic Citizen Kane.*

THE SHRILL CRY of an alarm clock suddenly shatters the silence. The footlights brighten and the heavy curtain rises to reveal the home of Bigger Thomas. An embattled youth in his late teens, he has little in common with the other black characters who have previously appeared in Broadway shows. He is not a song-and-dance man or a shuffling servant; nor is he onstage to offer a bit of comic relief or function as a token black amid an otherwise all-white cast. He is very human and very real.

Wright has cut Bigger from the fabric of his own life. Like his creator, Bigger has survived a childhood of extreme poverty in the racially discriminatory South and has fled to the North, where all black Americans are supposed to have greater opportunities awaiting them. Yet he is disappointed to find that a subtler, though equally powerful, form of discrimination is present in this part of the country.

Bigger's sense of disappointment is captured onstage by the squalid apartment he shares with his family. The plastered walls are cracked and spotted with water stains from leaky pipes. Laundry is draped over the shabby furniture. A rusty iron bed is positioned in the far corner. A pile of quilts sits in the middle of the floor.

The ringing alarm clock rouses Bigger's mother and his sister, Vera, from the bed. It also awakens Bigger and his younger brother, Buddy, who are nestled beneath the quilts on the floor. The Thomas family arises and prepares for breakfast.

Suddenly, Bigger and Buddy spy a huge, menacing rat. Bigger arms himself with a frying pan and stalks the animal. When the rat pauses, Bigger raises the pan above his head and summons his strength. Then he brings down the pan and smashes the rat. As the other members of Bigger's family look on in horror and disgust, he bashes the creature again and again. He seems to delight in the killing, experiencing a

feeling of power and a sense of control he has never felt before.

The morning newspapers on March 26, 1941, carry glowing reviews of the play. "Mr. Wright and Paul Green have written a powerful drama," the *New York Times* says, "and Orson Welles has staged it with imagination and force." Lee's performance, which expertly communicates the complex emotions that tear at the heart of the rebellious Bigger Thomas, is hailed as well.

Native Son was one of the first Broadway shows to examine the realities of life in a black ghetto. In the original cast, the Thomas family was played by (from left to right) Evelyn Ellis (as Hannah), Canada Lee (as Bigger), Lloyd Warren (as Buddy), and Helen Martin (as Vera).

The dynamic staging of Native Son *helped the 1941 Broadway production achieve, according to the New York Post, "the almost unbearable suspense of Wright's novel." The play closed in New York for the summer and re-opened several months later at the Apollo Theater in the black up-town district of Harlem.*

Also praised is Welles's imaginative staging. The *Daily Worker* reports, "In comparison, all the productions of the current season seem dim." Full of jarring city noises and sweeping beams of light, the theatrical effects help the play achieve the terror and unbearable suspense that is present in the novel.

But most important, the reviewers let it be known that they have heard Wright's powerful message loudly and clearly. They have anguished with Bigger through the murder he ultimately commits, through his panic and mute confusion, and through his eventual sentencing to die in the electric chair. Wright's painful story of racial oppression, brilliantly staged for a public that has long avoided the issue, is pronounced by the critics as "the biggest American drama of the season."

Like the book, the stage version of *Native Son* makes it clear that white society is largely responsible for turning blacks like Bigger into criminals. When a society refuses to grant full rights to each of its individuals—when it denies them jobs and an education—then that society creates a being who is inhuman. It is a message that Wright longs to bring to everyone who will listen to him. "I hope," he tells a luncheon group gathered to honor him in New York, "you will all have a chance to meet Bigger Thomas."

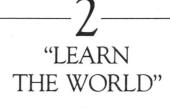

2
"LEARN
THE WORLD"

RICHARD NATHANIEL WRIGHT was born on September 4, 1908, in Adams County, Mississippi, and spent his early years in a ramshackle house on a large plantation 25 miles north of Natchez. It was, he recalled in *Black Boy*, an account of his childhood, a thickly wooded region of great natural beauty. "There was the delight I caught in seeing long straight rows of red and green vegetables stretching away in the sun to the bright horizon," he said. "There was the faint, cool kiss of sensuality when dew came on to my cheeks and shins as I ran down the wet green garden paths in the early morning."

Little else about Wright's youth was idyllic, however. Although southwestern Mississippi had an inviting landscape, it was, for its black inhabitants, one of the most destitute areas in the nation. Rigidly enforced Jim Crow laws separated blacks from white society and made them second-class citizens. Without exception, they were denied all opportunities for advancement and were forced to endure tremendous hardships.

Richard's parents, like most blacks who farmed in the South after the Civil War, scratched out a living as sharecroppers. Nathan Wright and his wife,

Wright spent his early years on a sharecropper's farm much like the one shown here. The southwest region of Mississippi in which he grew up was one of the poorest parts of the entire country.

21

Natchez Under the Hill—the poor side of the Mississippi river town that Wright visited during his youth—shown here around the time of his birth.

the former Ella Wilson, had arranged with a local landowner to tend his wide, flat fields of neatly planted cotton in return for a cabin, supplies, and a portion of the money that the crops yielded. Relying on cotton as a cash crop was usually not very lucrative, however, for cotton depleted the soil with each passing season.

Richard's mother, a schoolteacher at Tates Magnolia Baptist Church, also worked in the cotton fields to help her husband keep the farm going. Although she was physically frail, she tended to view her various ailments as tests of her will and faith. She was fiercely religious and saw to it that Richard went with her to church.

When Richard was four years old, his father decided to give up the grueling labor and constant debt that plagued the life of a sharecropper. He prepared his family for a move by boat to Memphis, one of Tennessee's largest commercial centers. By then, the family included two-year-old Leon, who rode up the gangplank atop a shabby suitcase.

Waving a hopeful farewell to Natchez, the Wrights lifted their belongings on board the *Kate Adams*, one of the South's last paddle-wheel riverboats, and watched it churn its way up the yellow

Mississippi River. As soon as the family arrived in Memphis, Nathan rented two small rooms in a squalid part of town and began to search for work. Yet he had a difficult time finding a job, and being illiterate did not help. Ella was unable to find a teaching job as well.

Richard also had a hard time adjusting to Memphis; its urban environment brought a great many changes to his life. No longer was he surrounded by the landscape of quiet beauty that had been his world since birth. Instead, his new landscape was cast in concrete, bounded by buildings, and peopled with tough characters. "The absence of green, growing things made the city seem dead," he said.

The first time Richard ventured out to the local grocery store in Memphis, he was robbed by a group of neighborhood boys and returned home beaten and humiliated. Ella, not one to coddle or comfort, insisted he go right back to the store and fight the boys for his money. Richard did as he was told.

A common sight throughout Wright's childhood: southern blacks bringing a bale of cotton to market. Wright's parents met with little success as sharecroppers farming the cotton fields of Mississippi.

Wright attended the Howe Institute, a small black grammar school in Memphis, Tennessee, when he was eight years old. An advertisement for the school is shown on the opposite page.

Nathan was not nearly as successful in meeting his obligations. He continued to have hard luck finding work, and as time passed, he became increasingly frustrated at his inability to land a job. He began to drink heavily and spend a great deal of time away from home. Two years after he arrived in Memphis, he abandoned his wife and children.

With his father gone, Richard often had to go through the day without food. "Hunger had always been more or less at my elbow when I played, but now I began to wake up at night to find hunger standing at my bedside, staring at me gauntly," he wrote in *Black Boy*. He ate only when his mother was healthy enough to take on menial jobs, which was the only kind of work available to blacks in the South.

Richard's lone distraction from the painful throes of hunger was the world of books. Encouraged by his mother, who liked to tell him stories and who taught him to read, he abandoned himself to the riches of literature. In fact, as he got older and went to school, he read practically all of the time, even during recess.

But there was no way for Richard to avoid certain unforeseen circumstances. In 1915, Ella suddenly became ill and found it necessary to place him and his brother in the Settlement House, a Methodist orphanage. This temporary refuge was, Wright wrote in *Black Boy*, a nightmarish hall crowded with noisy, hungry children.

Each morning, Richard and the others were herded outside to pull weeds from the lawn. "Many mornings I was too weak from hunger to pull the grass," he said, recalling that the two daily meals consisted of only a slice of bread with molasses. "I would grow dizzy and my mind would become blank and I would find myself, after an interval of unconsciousness, upon my hands and knees, my head whirling, my eyes staring in bleak astonishment at the green grass, wondering where I was, feeling that I was emerging from a dream." When Richard ran away from the Settlement House six weeks after he arrived, Ella promptly removed her two boys from the orphanage.

In 1916, Wright began his formal education at the Howe Institute, a small, segregated neighborhood grammar school. During his first few weeks there, he was overcome by shyness: He was ashamed of his lack of schooling as well as his shoddy clothing. Yet he had a naturally quick mind and was an eager reader, and within a few months he caught up to his classmates.

The Howe Institute, like most of the schools that blacks attended in the racially segregated South during the early part of the 20th century, did not receive a fair share of financial support from the state government. Instead, the majority of funds that each state earmarked for public education went to schools for whites. As a result, the Howe Institute remained

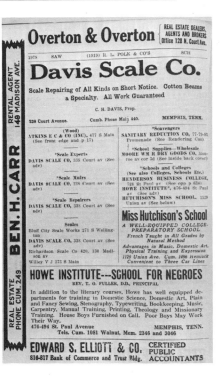

Wright lived at various times throughout his youth with his maternal grandmother, whose rigid moral outlook contributed to his rebelliousness.

open by relying on tuition fees and looking to its supporters for charitable contributions.

As it turned out, Richard was unable to complete the school year. His mother became ill again, and he had to withdraw from class because she could not pay his tuition. To ease matters, the family returned to Adams County and stayed with one of Nathan's brothers. The following year, they went to Elaine, Arkansas, to stay with Ella's sister, Maggie, and her husband, Silas Hoskins, who owned a successful saloon that served the black workers from nearby sawmills.

When Ella and her two boys stepped off the train at the Elaine station in 1918, summer was all around them. They carried their bags happily toward Maggie's house, listening to the bees hum in the brilliant wildflowers that grew along the clay road. To Richard, life at the Hoskins residence was luxurious. Mealtimes brought an unfamiliar sight: plates piled unbelievably high with meat and biscuits. The constant flow of cold, fresh milk gave him, he said, a "drugged, sleepy feeling that came from . . . drinking enough for the first time in my life."

Richard's stay in the town of Elaine was brief, however. One autumn morning, his Uncle Silas failed to return from the saloon. (To protect his property, Silas usually slept in the tavern overnight, with a revolver close at hand, and returned home at daybreak.) The family paced in silence all day long, until they heard a knock at the door. A young black man stood on the porch, clenching his hat in his hands. He told them in a solemn voice that Silas had been murdered by several white men who coveted the saloonkeeper's flourishing business. Moreover, these men were now threatening to kill Silas's entire family. Maggie and Ella promptly rounded up the boys and a few necessities and fled to nearby West Helena, Arkansas.

Trouble soon struck again: Richard's mother suffered a stroke that left her partially paralyzed. His maternal grandmother came from Jackson, Mississippi, to fetch Ella and the children. Taking care of three additional people proved to be too much of a burden to Richard's grandmother, however, and she was forced to send the children to live with other relatives. Leon went to stay with Maggie, who had relocated to Detroit, and Richard went to stay with his Aunt Jody and Uncle Clark in Greenwood, Mississippi, about 80 miles north of Jackson.

Shortly after Richard returned to his grandmother's home in 1920, he began attending the Jim Hill Public School. Even though he had not yet completed one full year of school, he had already done a great deal of reading, and his innate cleverness propelled him to the top of his class. In 1923, he entered the Smith-Robertson Public School, a two-year junior high school for blacks. To help pay for his school-books and clothing, he took a job as a handyman for a white family and spent several hours each day before and after school as their chauffeur, gardener, and housecleaner.

Wright continued to be an avid reader and an enthusiastic pupil at Smith-Robertson. He often volunteered to give a report to his classmates on a newspaper or magazine article he had read. Among the periodicals he liked to read were black newspapers such as the *Chicago Defender* and the *Pittsburgh Courier*. He also read the *Crisis*, which was published by the nation's leading antidiscrimination organization, the National Asssociation for the Advancement of Colored People (NAACP).

Although Richard proved to be an excellent student, the trying times of his youth also made him independent and stubborn, and school officials occasionally found him troublesome. He came to realize, he said, "that there were feelings denied me,

Wright enrolled in the Jim Hill Public School in Jackson, Mississippi, when he was 12 years old and remained there for the entire academic year. This was the first time in his life that he did not have to move to another town before the school year came to an end.

that the very breath of life itself was beyond my reach," and he angrily refused to put on what he called "the artificial status of race and class"—the pretense of humility that whites expected blacks to display before figures of authority. One time, he even refused to pray with his classmates for an end to a terrible drought, claiming God had "no influence over the cycle of water in nature." Instead, he sat rigidly at his desk while the rest of the class rose in prayer.

Wright had already rejected the religious fanaticism of his grandmother and his aunt Addie, who were Seventh-Day Adventists, a religious sect that stresses the Second Coming of Jesus Christ and the Last Judgment. They not only read constantly from the Bible and prayed daily but also did their best to make Richard follow suit. When they refused to let him work on Saturdays in observance of the Sabbath, he told them he would run away from home if they did not stop trying to control his life.

"Was I really as bad as my uncles and aunts and Granny repeatedly said?" Wright asked in *Black Boy*. "It was inconceivable to me that one should surrender to what seemed wrong, and most of the people I had met seemed wrong. Ought one to surrender to authority even if one believed that authority was wrong? If the answer was yes, then I knew that I would always be wrong, because I could never do it."

Wright chose to escape from his impoverished world in another way. One afternoon in the autumn of 1923, while he was in the eighth grade, he eased his dreamy boredom in class by sketching out the plot of a story in which a villainous man tries to swindle a helpless widow out of her house. Within three days, he had worked "The Voodoo of Hell's Half Acre" into a finished short story.

Excited and confident, Richard marched into the offices of the *Southern Register*, a black weekly newspaper started by editor Malcolm D. Rogers. Richard held out the dog-eared composition book that contained "The Voodoo of Hell's Half Acre" and insisted that Rogers read the story. After doing so, the editor agreed to print it in three installments. The story was published in early 1924, and its acceptance led Wright to a powerful dream: Someday, he would leave the South and all its restrictions behind and become a successful writer.

At the age of 15, Richard had already seen that southern blacks were assigned what he called the "role of non-men." There was no way for them to improve their life. It was dangerous for them to be forthright and proud. And, as he had witnessed so clearly in the case of his uncle Silas, it was dangerous for them to be successful. Lynchings, a form of white vigilantism intended to maintain racial supremacy, were common in the South.

"Somewhere in the dead of the southern night," Wright wrote in *Black Boy*, "my life had switched onto the wrong track and, without my knowing it, the locomotive of my heart was rushing down a dangerously steep slope, heading for a collision, heedless of the warning red lights that blinked all about me, the sirens and the bells and the screams that filled the air." He believed he must escape to the North if he wanted to keep alive his hopes for accomplishment and make something of himself. He had to leave the South before either his dreams were killed or he was killed because of his dreams.

Richard still had one more year to complete at Smith-Robertson before he could leave the South, and it turned out to be a lonely year. While some of his fellow classmates chattered gaily about which high school they planned on attending next, he was unable to share in their excitement. His family, often forced to eat daily meals of mush, lard, and gravy, could barely afford to pay the rent, let alone send him to

high school. They were anxious for him to leave school so he could find a full-time job and bring more money into the household.

As the school year came to an end, Richard, about to graduate first among the 30 students in his class, was pronounced the valedictorian. With this honor came an assignment to write and deliver a speech at the school's graduation ceremony. Several days after he was told about the assignment, he was called into the office of the school principal, a man named Lanier. Richard strode proudly through the office door, only to have Lanier slap down a sheaf of stapled pages and push them across his wide desk.

"Well, Richard Wright, there's your speech," the principal said.

The teenager was dumbfounded. Why should the principal give him a speech? Richard had already spent many hours outlining his talk. He had titled it "The Attributes of Life," and it addressed the edu-

Wright lived in Jackson, the largest city in Mississippi, from 1920 to 1925. He later wrote in Black Boy: A Record of Childhood and Youth *that it was in Jackson that he first realized how deeply the racist attitudes of whites affected black life in the South.*

Wright stood apart from his fellow classmates while in junior high at the Smith-Robertson Public School in Jackson, Mississippi: He read widely, published a short story in a local newspaper, and ultimately graduated first in his class. "My deepest instinct," he said later, "has always made me reject the 'place' the white South had assigned me."

cational system of the South and how it deprived black children of their intellectual freedom. Richard had plenty to say, and he did not need the principal to help him say it.

Lanier was insistent, however. He had invited several top-level administrators as well as several local politicians to the commencement ceremony, and he did not want to risk having Wright offend anyone. Lanier demanded that the ninth grader read the prepared speech.

Burning with rage, Richard shoved the papers back across Lanier's desk. "I know I'm not educated, Professor," he said, "but the people are coming here to hear the students, and I won't make a speech that you've written."

They argued bitterly, back and forth, until the principal threatened to keep Richard from graduating altogether. The young man called the principal's bluff and threatened to quit school at once. Lanier tried to reason with him.

"You're just a young, hot fool," he said. "Wake up, boy. Learn the world you're living in. If you play it safe," he smiled and winked, "I'll help you go to college."

Richard could not be cajoled. He was determined to read his own words despite the pleas that came from his classmates, teachers, and relatives in the days that followed.

On May 29, 1925, Wright stood tensely before the sea of white and black faces that filled the school auditorium. He delivered his own speech. "When my voice stopped there was some applause," he said later. "I did not care if they liked it or not; I was through. Immediately, even before I left the platform, I tried to shunt all memory of the event from me."

What had seemed to be an important moral victory left Wright isolated and saddened. The day seemed to be a forbidding preview of the adult life he was about to begin. "A few of my classmates managed to shake my hand as I pushed toward the door, seeking the street," he recalled. "Somebody invited me to a party and I did not accept. I did not want to see any of them again. I walked home, saying to myself: The hell with it! With almost seventeen years of baffled living behind me, I faced the world in 1925." ❧

3

AN UNSEEN LIGHT

EARLY IN THE summer of 1925, Wright began to hunt for full-time work. He quickly discovered that job discrimination was so prevalent in the South it evoked the days of slave labor, which had come to an end nearly a half century earlier. No matter how well educated blacks were, they were denied good positions chiefly because white employers refused to hire black workers for important jobs. Instead, they were offered only unskilled posts.

Sadly, the education Wright had received at the Smith-Robertson School had not prepared him for his entrance into Mississippi's working world. He had not learned at school that he was supposed to hide his high degree of intelligence from his white bosses. Nor was he willing to assume the humble and deferential demeanor that whites expected of blacks. Yet he was determined to make enough money to finance a trip to the North, and that meant he had to find a job and stick with it no matter how menial the position might be.

Eventually, Wright was hired as a porter in Farley's clothing store. Most of Farley's customers were black residents of Jackson who bought their suits and dresses on credit. The small weekly payments they

Blacks march in the nation's capital in 1922 to protest white vigilantism in the United States. The violence that often befell blacks in the South became a dominant theme in Wright's early fiction.

wound up making on the garments usually added up to much more than the items of clothing were actually worth.

One morning as Wright knelt on the sidewalk, polishing the brass knobs of the store's front doors, Farley's long, shiny car pulled up to the curb. Inside the car, a black woman sat between the store owner and his son. Suddenly, the car doors flew open and the woman was pushed onto the street by the Farleys. Then they started to shove her roughly toward the back entrance of the store. From across the street, a white policeman watched without expression.

Wright resumed his polishing. Some minutes later, he saw the woman stumble out of the store. Crying and bleeding badly, she tried to pull her ripped clothing close around her. The policeman approached her and asked her a few questions. Then he arrested her for drunkenness.

After Wright watched the patrol car take the woman away, he went inside, bewildered by what had happened. His coworkers soon set him straight. They told him that a beating like the one the woman had received from the Farleys was a routine procedure. It was their way of discouraging late payments on their clothing.

A few weeks later, Wright was faced with another frightening, racially motivated incident. He had just delivered an item purchased at Farley's to a customer several miles away and was in the process of riding back to town when one of the tires on his bicycle went flat. He dismounted the bike and started to walk with it along the edge of the dusty road. Before long, he felt the midday sun blazing overhead and realized that his sweating palms were barely able to grip the handlebars. The heat was very tiring.

Wright turned his head and saw a carful of young white men slow down alongside him. "Hop on to the running board," the driver called out. Wright gratefully scrambled aboard, pulling up the disabled bicycle after him.

As the car rolled along at a fast speed, Wright noticed that the men were passing a whiskey flask among themselves. One of them grinned and held the flask out the window, offering it to Wright. He gave a little laugh but declined, telling the man, "Oh, no, thanks."

No sooner were the words out of Wright's mouth than he felt a smashing blow to the side of his head. He slumped and tumbled off the running board, the bicycle clattering behind him. A hurled whiskey bottled crashed onto the road beside him. As the car sped away, he heard someone from the car shout at him, "You better learn to say 'sir' to a white man."

To Wright, who was well aware of the dictum of white supremacy in the South, it seemed futile to fight against the brutal treatment he and other blacks received. Nevertheless, he was unable to mask his feelings and look cheerful whenever a confrontation took place. Such was the case one day when he sat in Farley's back room, reading as usual during his lunch break. Looking up from his book, he noticed that Farley's son was glowering at him.

"Why don't you laugh and talk like the others?" the young man demanded.

Wright tried to keep a polite voice as he answered firmly, "Well, sir, there's nothing much to say or smile about."

Farley's son whirled off in a huff and returned minutes later, clutching a few dollar bills that he angrily tossed at Wright. "I don't like your looks," young Farley snapped. "Now get out."

After Wright was dismissed from his job at the clothing store, he started to fear he would never get out of the South. Jobs for unskilled blacks were not only low paying but scarce. Moreover, most of the money he made was claimed by his family. His

Wright returned to Memphis, Tennessee, in 1925, more than a decade after he was abandoned there by his father. The 17-year-old Wright's arrival in this thriving southern city marked the beginning of his attempt to reach, he said, "a land where I could live with a little less fear."

younger brother contributed little financial support. Like Richard, Leon had been deprived of proper nourishment as a child; consequently, he was sickly and was rarely able to work.

Wright enrolled in Lanier High School in the fall of 1925, the same year that it became the first black public high school to open in Jackson. He did not remain there for very long, however. By late autumn, he had decided to take whatever savings he had amassed and leave town.

Wright filled a small suitcase with a pair of new shoes and a few pieces of clothing, then kissed his mother good-bye and promised to send for her and Leon as soon as possible. Around midnight, a long, thin whistle sounded as he boarded a northbound train. His first destination was Memphis, Tennessee.

It was a cool November morning when Wright arrived in Memphis, a teeming, river-port city of about 160,000 people. He walked cautiously along the downtown streets, looking in all directions at once, mindful of the city's reputation for pickpockets and thugs. Heading down Beale Street, he passed the billiard parlors and jazz cafés whose back rooms were stacked with cases of illicit bathtub gin. The Eighteenth Amendment to the U.S. Constitution, ratified in 1919, had made it illegal to manufacture, transport, or sell alcoholic beverages in the United States.

At 570 Beale, Wright paused in front of a large white house that advertised rooms for rent. He went to knock on the door and was greeted by the proprietor of the rooming house, who introduced herself as Mrs. Moss. Her wide smile and easygoing manner quickly won him over. She spoke with a great deal of warmth and tenderness—qualities he seldom encountered among his own troubled family.

Along with her husband and daughter, Bess, Mrs. Moss made a home for the 17-year-old itinerant that he would never forget. The tensions and humiliations he had felt at his last job quickly faded; the hunger and poverty he had known while living with his mother and Leon were soon forgotten. At last, he felt, he was in a secure and loving home. "I lay on the bed," he recalled, "and reveled in the delightful sensation of living out a long-sought dream. . . . I could start anew."

Wright soon found work as a dishwasher at Lyle's Drugstore. Because the job included two free meals a day, he was able to save a little extra from his salary of $10 per week. He worked next as an errand boy for the Merry Optical Company, washing eyeglasses and carrying light packages to the post office. During lunchtime, he earned extra money by running small errands for some of the employees.

Throughout his two-year stay in Memphis, Wright kept to an extremely strict budget in an attempt to save money. In addition to working at lunchtime to pocket some extra change, he walked to and from work rather than take public transportation, and he ate as sparingly as he could. By now, he had learned how to get by with very little, and being in a state of hunger had become an accustomed way of life.

Wright's only real indulgence was books and magazines. He liked to browse at the city's secondhand bookshops, where he discovered such well-regarded magazines as *Harper's*, *Atlantic Monthly*, and *American Mercury*. He bought used magazines for a few pennies each and read them carefully before selling them back to the shop owners.

Every morning before work, Wright stopped at the lobby of a nearby bank building and read a copy of the Memphis *Commercial Appeal*, a daily newspaper. One morning in May 1927, when he came across an editorial in the paper that attacked the ideas of the southern writer H. L. Mencken, he felt what he later described as a "tinge of warmth from an unseen light." Mencken, as editor in chief of the *American Mercury*, often railed against racial prejudice in the South. The editorial in the *Commercial Appeal* blasted what it called his "foolish" notions of society.

Wright was stunned to see such hostile words directed at a white man. The editorial not only stirred Wright's sympathy. It gave him hope that there were other men—white as well as black—who despised the iniquities of the South.

Wright became determined to get his hands on all of Mencken's writings to find out why his ideas met with such harsh criticism. But this was not an easy task. The Memphis public library system did not allow blacks to check out books.

Wright decided to take a bold step. He approached a fellow employee named Falk, who was often taunted by the other workers because he was an Irish Catholic. Wright hoped that Falk, who knew what it felt like to be subjected to prejudice, would do a favor for him. He asked the Irishman if he could borrow his library card, and Falk agreed—on the condition that Wright did not let anyone know about their arrangement.

Later that day, Wright anxiously presented himself to the local librarian. She looked at the young black man who stood humbly before her and then at the note she had been handed. Wright had forged the message on the note, which read: *Dear Madam: Will you please let this nigger boy have some books by*

No man of letters had a more profound effect on Wright's literary career than the southern editor H. L. Mencken (center, holding his magazine, The American Mercury). *After reading Mencken's* A Book of Prefaces, *Wright realized, "This man was fighting, fighting with words. He was using words as a weapon, using them as one would use a club. Could words be weapons? Well, yes, for here they were. Then, maybe, perhaps, I could use them as a weapon?"*

The writings of Theodore Dreiser, the author of such naturalistic novels as An American Tragedy *and* Sister Carrie, *also had a powerful influence on Wright. "All my life,"* Wright noted in Black Boy, *"had shaped me for the realism, the naturalism of the modern novel."*

H. L. Mencken? After some deliberation, the librarian rounded up several books, including Mencken's *A Book of Prefaces*, which is an introduction to the writings of many 20th-century novelists.

Wright sat up all night poring over Mencken's prose. He was mesmerized by Mencken's use of language—the noted author brandished words as though they were weapons—and amazed by the courage it must have taken to write that way. He pictured Mencken slashing with his pen at the follies of society, shredding racial prejudice, greed, and human weaknesses, and he wondered whether he could do it, too.

Wright was also fascinated by Mencken's discussion of a number of writers. Who were these men whom Mencken spoke about with such passion: Joseph Conrad, Fyodor Dostoyevski, Edgar Allan Poe, Leo Tolstoy, Mark Twain? And what kinds of books did they write?

Wright soon found out. His imagination was so stirred by Mencken that reading these authors became a nightly passion. Every book he read gave him an added perspective on life and expanded his rather limited view of the world. "It was not," he said later, "a matter of believing or disbelieving what I read, but of feeling something new, of being affected by something that made the look of the world different."

Before long, the 19-year-old Wright developed a new kind of hunger: a hunger for knowledge. He took out books by such contemporary writers as Theodore Dreiser, Sherwood Anderson, and Sinclair Lewis, who used their novels to analyze the ills of society. Their works also inspired him, and night after night he tried to copy their literary style. Unfortunately, his own efforts at writing fell flat.

By the fall of 1927, Wright had saved enough money to move to a larger residence and summon his family. Leon and Ella, who was still in uncertain health, arrived within days at Richard's small apartment on Washington Street, not far from the burlesque houses and blues halls of Beale Street. Shortly after the family was reunited, Aunt Maggie came to join them. She had just separated from her second husband and was anxious to start a new life in the North. Her energy and enthusiasm spurred the family into deciding that she and her oldest nephew should leave right away by train for Chicago. Ella and Leon would follow as soon as Richard saved enough money to send for them.

Wright's expectations were extremely high. "I was leaving the South to fling myself into the unknown, to meet other situations that would perhaps elicit from me other responses," he said. "And if I could meet enough of a different life, then, perhaps, gradually and slowly I might learn who I was, what I might be."

It was, Wright realized, a circuitous journey. "I was not leaving the South to forget the South," he said, "but so that some day I might understand it." ❧

4
FISTS
OF REVOLT

❦

WRIGHT WAS HARDLY encouraged by his first glimpse of Chicago. As his train slowed down near Union Station in November 1927, he saw the city stretched out before him. Long brown warehouses covered most of the surrounding blocks. Yellowish steam billowed from factory smokestacks and hung heavily in the air. "The din of the city," he wrote in *American Hunger*, "entered my consciousness, entered to remain for years to come. . . ." Aunt Maggie, seated next to him, rested her head against the back of the worn velvet train seat and closed her eyes.

Home to some 3 million inhabitants, Chicago was a fast-paced city that was still growing rapidly. Most of the newcomers were blacks from the South. Like Wright, they were seeking the benefits of a metropolis that boasted its own black neighborhoods, stores, newspapers, and political leaders.

As Wright walked through the station, he failed to see any of the For Whites Only signs that were so prevalent in other parts of the country. When he boarded a bus to take him to the home of Maggie's

Chicago was home to Wright from 1927 to 1937. He said of black life in the North, "We live amid swarms of people, yet there is a vast distance between people. . . . In the South life was different; men spoke to you, cursed you, yelled at you, or killed you. The world moved by signs we knew. But here in the North cold forces hit you and push you."

U.S. postal workers sorting mail in 1930. While Wright was employed at the Chicago post office, he made a number of friends who belonged to the American Communist party and encouraged him to become a party member.

aunt Cleo, he stared at the other passengers in amazement. Blacks and whites sat side by side.

Shortly after Wright settled in Cleo's small apartment, he landed a job and sent for Ella and Leon. During the next two years, he worked as a dishwasher and a delivery boy. He enrolled at Englewood High School but left after it became clear that he was much better read than the other students.

In the spring of 1928, Wright took a civil service examination and became a substitute worker at the Chicago post office. When each workday ended, he hurried home to record his on-the-job experiences. Many of these observations eventually made their way into his novel *Lawd Today*.

Although it was published posthumously in 1963, *Lawd Today* was actually the first novel Wright ever wrote. The title, he said, was "a folk exclamation on confronting the events of the day . . . to express a people who have not been able to make their life their own, who must live 'from day to day.' " The book examines a single day in the life of a common laborer named Jake Jackson and describes the oppressive conditions that Wright himself confronted at the post office: the drudgery of mail sorting, the noise of the stamping machines, the severe, prison-like atmosphere.

Despite these dreary conditions, a postal worker's pay was fairly decent and his workday was relatively short. As a result, Wright became upset when he failed a medical exam to become a permanent employee. Even though he had stuffed himself with 2 quarts of buttermilk and 6 bananas on the morning of the physical, his weight did not meet the required 125-pound minimum. He was of average height, but his frame had failed to fill out after so many years of near starvation.

More bad news for Wright followed. As he was walking home from the public library one evening in October 1929, he stopped at a newsstand and stared at a shocking headline: STOCKS CRASH—BILLIONS FADE. The sudden collapse of the New York Stock Exchange, marking the start of the Great Depression, plunged the entire country into economic chaos and deep panic. Within days of the crash, the volume of mail decreased so dramatically at the post office that Wright's hours were cut in half. His paycheck was reduced as well, and he and his family, like countless other Americans, got much of their food by standing on breadlines at public relief kitchens.

None of Wright's subsequent jobs lasted for very long. His brief stint with an insurance company was followed by vote-gathering roles with both the Republican and the Democratic parties. These unchallenging work experiences accentuated the negative aspects of all his previous jobs, including the one at the post office, and helped him identify more than

A Chicago breadline in 1930. Throughout the Great Depression, thousands of Americans, including Wright and his family, were forced to rely on relief kitchens for their meals.

ever with the unhappy plight of other proletarian laborers.

In the spring of 1930, when Wright was temporarily out of work, he spent part of his time walking through one of the city's public areas, Washington Park. Occasionally, he stopped to listen to some of the many public speakers who stood on soapboxes to discuss the worsening depression with an audience of unemployed blacks. Fed up with their situation, the people were eager to hear about any prospects of social change.

Most of the speakers were American Communist party members expounding their remedies for the current economic crisis. They told their listeners that hundreds of ghetto families were being evicted from their homes each month because they were unable to pay their rent during this time of widespread unemployment. In response to this development, the Communist party had organized the League of Struggle for Negro Rights, with league members staging massive protests against the evictions. The Communist party, the speakers said to the crowd, believed in racial equality and actively demonstrated against prejudice.

A sense of grass-roots power filled the air as the exhortatory speeches created feelings of unity and brotherhood among the unemployed workers. For the poor of the 1930s, especially the black poor, who wanted to make their voices heard, joining the Communist party seemed like a highly attractive option. In fact, it was just about their only alternative for political representation. Their opinions counted for very little in shaping the policies of either the Democratic or the Republican party, especially in the South, where many voting-age blacks were unable to cast a ballot because of discriminatory state laws that required them to pass a literacy test.

One Saturday, Wright crossed paths with "Billy Goat" Brown, a soapbox orator who attacked most aspects of American society, including the fact that whites wielded virtually all of the power in the nation. He must be crazy, Wright told himself. He had read books in which H. L. Mencken insulted the South, but he had never heard another man speak out so publicly and so passionately against the whites in America.

"I was slowly beginning to comprehend the meaning of my environment," Wright said of this period

A meeting of the American Communist party in the early 1930s. The party, in attempting to address a wide variety of society's ills, looked to writers such as Wright to help voice its views.

in Chicago. "A sense of direction was beginning to emerge from the conditions of my life. I began to feel something more powerful than I could express. My speech and manner changed. My cynicism slid from me. I grew open and questioning. I wanted to know."

There was one thing about Wright that did not change, however; he kept alive his determination to become a successful writer. In 1931, seven years after seeing "The Voodoo of Hell's Half Acre" in print, he published his second short story, "Superstition." A gothic tale of multiple murders at a family reunion, it appeared in the April 1931 issue of *Abbott's Monthly* magazine, which was geared to the city's large black population.

In 1932, a social worker who was assisting the Wright household invited Richard to a meeting of the John Reed Club, an organization established at the onset of the depression to bring together artists, writers, and intellectuals who held radical views and shared an interest in correcting the ills of society. The Communist party sponsored the John Reed Club, which was named after the American journalist who reported on the Russian revolution and wrote about the events in the best-selling book *Ten Days That Shook the World.* By the early 1930s, branches of the organization were located throughout the United States.

Wright was uncertain at first about joining the John Reed Club. Around the time that he went to his first meeting, only about 5 percent of the organization's 16,000 members were black. It appeared to him that the Communist party and the John Reed Club, among whose members in Chicago were the writer Nelson Algren and the painter Jackson Pollock, were not as dedicated to helping blacks as he had been led to believe by the speakers in Washington Park.

The communist literature Wright was handed at the meeting changed his mind about the organization's goals. These tracts, which prompted him to read other extremist works, including the political philosopher and socialist Karl Marx's *Communist Manifesto* and *Das Kapital*, helped him realize that blacks were not alone in being poor and oppressed (both in the United States and abroad) and that their participation in the John Reed Club was truly necessary. Without any further hesitation, he joined the John Reed Club and the Communist party. "It seemed to me," he wrote in *American Hunger*, "that here at last in the realm of the revolutionary expression was where Negro experience could find a home, a functioning of value and role."

Journalist John Reed's book Ten Days That Shook the World *was an eyewitness account of the 1917 Bolshevik revolution that helped spur the rise of the Communist party in the United States. The party honored Reed in 1929 by sponsoring the John Reed Club, an organization for radical artists and intellectuals, of which Wright became a member.*

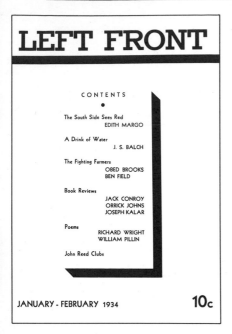

LEFT FRONT

CONTENTS
•

The South Side Sees Red
EDITH MARGO

A Drink of Water
J. S. BALCH

The Fighting Farmers
OBED BROOKS
BEN FIELD

Book Reviews
JACK CONROY
ORRICK JOHNS
JOSEPH KALAR

Poems
RICHARD WRIGHT
WILLIAM PILLIN

John Reed Clubs

JANUARY - FEBRUARY 1934   **10c**

*Left Front was a literary maga-
zine published by the John Reed
Club. The January–February
1934 issue of this left-wing journal included two of Wright's ear-
liest protest poems, "Rest for the
Weary" and "A Red Love Note."*

As it turned out, Wright served the purposes of the John Reed Club just as much as the Communist party suited his own particular needs. The Chicago chapter of the party was on the lookout for young writers—especially young, poor, and militant black writers—to contribute to its literary magazine, *Left Front*, and Richard Wright clearly fit the description of an oppressed black who had the makings of a strong black spokesman for the Communist party. He began to write with increased energy and enthusiasm once he became a party member, "feeling for the first time," he said, "that I could speak to listening ears."

In the January–February 1934 issue of *Left Front*, Wright published two radical poems: "Rest for the Weary" and "A Red Love Note." Several months later, the leftist journal *New Masses* printed his poem "I Have Seen Black Hands." It was to become one of his best-known pieces of political verse. Strongly emotional and rich in revolutionary spirit, it expresses the hope that the Commmunist party will bring about racial equality. The poem concludes with the lines:

> I am black and I have seen black hands
> Raised in fists of revolt, side by side with the white
> fists of white workers
> And some day—and it is this only which sustains me—
> Some day there shall be millions and millions of
> them
> On some red day in a burst of fists on a new horizon.

The John Reed Club opened up a new world to Wright. He made many new acquaintances and spent his evenings discussing politics and writing. Two friends in particular, Joyce Gourfain and her husband, Ed, suggested he counterbalance his newfound fascination with Marxist theory by reading the works of such prominent modern writers as T. S. Eliot, William Faulkner, and Gertrude Stein. Wright, always an avid reader, complied by reading everyone from Stephen Crane and Ernest Hemingway to James Joyce and Marcel Proust, whose *Remembrance of Things Past* "crushed me with hopelessness," Wright said, "for I wanted to write of the people in my environment with an equal thoroughness, and the burning example before my eyes made me feel that I never could."

Wright spent part of this period working as an orderly in a hospital and supervising a South Side youth club for black males between the ages of 8 and 25. Raised in the ghetto, these youths were a wild and restless lot. "For hours I listened to their talk of planes, women, guns, politics, and crime," Wright said. "Their figures of speech were as forceful and colorful as any ever used by English-speaking people. I kept a pencil and paper in my pocket to jot down their word-rhythms and reactions." He later melded many of their phrases and what he called "their twisted dreams, their all too-clear destinies" into the voice and actions of Bigger Thomas, the hero of *Native Son*.

Wright's intellectual pursuits and work commitments did not stop him from sampling the delights of Chicago's South Side, the part of the city that

The Communist party had many supporters in Chicago during the 1930s, including the hundreds of demonstrators at this unemployment protest rally. Yet as the decade advanced, Wright became less and less enamored with the demands that the party made on him.

Chicago's chief black neighborhood, the South Side, offered its many black residents a real sense of community, yet it was hardly a paradise. Because the South Side became home to virtually all of the city's black migrants—including Wright—who were seeking refuge from the racially discriminatory South, overcrowding, poverty, and the indifference of the city government helped turn it into a run-down black ghetto.

boasted the second-largest black population in the nation (after Harlem, in New York). The many cabarets and clubs that lined the streets of the South Side were usually packed with black audiences anxious to hear the hot new sounds of jazz. New Orleans may have been the birthplace of jazz, but Chicago was where it evolved into a national sensation under bandleader Joe "King" Oliver (whose orchestra featured cornetist Louis Armstrong) in the 1920s. Musicians such as Armstrong and pianist Earl "Fatha" Hines helped the midwestern city remain a vital and popular jazz center throughout the following decade, when the South Side was displaced by Harlem as the jazz capital of America.

Wright also left his mark on Chicago, winning legions of admirers as Communist party magazines such as *The Anvil* and *International Literature* published more and more of his radical verse. In April 1935, his poem "Red Leaves of Red Books" appeared in *New Masses*. A striking example of his Marxist poetry, it implores blacks and whites to work together:

Turn
Red leaves of red books
Turn
In white palms and black palms
Turn
Slowly in the mute hours of the night
Turn
In the fingers of women and the fingers of men
In the fingers of the old and the fingers of the young.

Two months after "Red Leaves of Red Books" was published, the Communist party in Chicago asked Wright to serve as its delegate to the first American Writers' Congress, which was held in New York. The conference was held for members of the League of American Writers, which was established by the Communist party in 1934 to supplant the John Reed Club. Various chapters of the John Reed Club had become somewhat independent, and the Communist party desired greater control of its literary operations. It wanted its artists and writers to concentrate only on works that would further the party cause.

On a June morning in 1935, Wright viewed the majestic skyline of New York for the first time. He

The South Side may have been in decline while Wright was living there, but the neighborhood was not without its attractions. The community's large black population made it an inviting stop for a number of the nation's leading jazz musicians, chief among them cornetist Louis Armstrong (front row, third from right), who performed in the South Side's many nightclubs and cabarets.

During the 1930s, the concerns of oppressed Americans were addressed by a variety of organizations and institutions, including the League of Struggle for Negro Rights, which published the pamphlet shown above in November 1933, and the John Reed Club, which offered art classes (described in the brochure on the opposite page) with an emphasis on social issues.

was equally taken with the city's inhabitants. New Yorkers, he said, "walked with a quicker stride and seemed intent upon reaching some destination in a great hurry." He spent the rest of the morning gazing at the great theaters on Broadway and soaking up the grandeur of one of the country's leading music centers, Carnegie Hall. The abundance of art and culture in the city left him entranced.

Later in the day, when the opening session of the Writers' Congress had come to an end, Wright's impressions of New York changed. He was unable to find a hotel in midtown that accepted blacks. His luck was not any better in Harlem. There he inquired at one hotel and rooming house after another but was unable to find a vacancy. Finally, at the suggestion of a hotel clerk, he found a room at the Harlem YMCA.

The next day at the Writers' Congress, Wright became even more dispirited. A motion was made to disband the John Reed Club, and a debate began. The Communist party leaders argued that the artistic aspect of the John Reed Club distracted the members from their true work, which was to educate the masses about the upcoming social revolution.

Wright, on the other hand, believed his first duty was to develop as a writer. Although he shared the party's hopes for social equality, he was not ready to devote his entire life's work to the party. Accordingly, he stood up during the debate and pleaded for the continuation of the John Reed Club. He explained how important it was for young writers to feel the support of the clubs and to have the reading audience they provided.

Not one person in the crowd cheered or applauded Wright's speech. In fact, when his address came to an end, he sat down to utter silence. He watched the room fill with upraised hands when the vote to dissolve the club was called. And when the call came for those who disagreed with the proposal, his hand alone went up in opposition to the Communist party.

In the end, only a couple of positive things happened to Wright during his stay in New York. He delivered a speech, "The Isolation of the Negro Writer," to the League of American Writers. And he had the opportunity to meet two writers whom he greatly admired: Theodore Dreiser and James T. Farrell. Both men wrote in a highly naturalistic style, looking closely at the bleak side of life as well as the good. Their respective works, especially Dreiser's *An American Tragedy* and Farrell's *Studs Lonigan*, profoundly influenced Wright's own naturalistic approach to writing.

Wright was back in Chicago in the fall of 1935, when President Franklin D. Roosevelt created the Works Progress Administration (WPA), a federal work-relief agency that provided jobs to thousands of people who were unemployed because of the ravaging effects of the Great Depression. Wright found several temporary jobs through the WPA. After months of street-sweeping and ditch-digging assignments, he enrolled in the Federal Writers' Project, a newly created branch of the agency. Along with 350 other writers, including Saul Bellow and Ralph Ellison, he was assigned to perform research for a massive guidebook on Illinois. By helping to compile such works as a "Bibliography of Chicago Negroes," he drew a regular paycheck as a writer for the first time in his life.

The early part of 1936 was an unusually busy time for Wright. The WPA transferred him to the Federal Theatre Project, where he worked as a public relations writer. He also helped plan a writers' group for an upcoming National Negro Congress, a convention in which the Communist party took a strong interest. He formed a literary set, the South Side Writers' Group, which included Margaret Walker, whose first

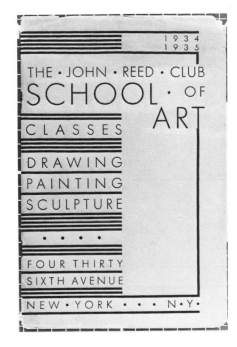

1934
1935
THE · JOHN · REED · CLUB
SCHOOL · OF
ART
CLASSES
DRAWING
PAINTING
SCULPTURE
· · · ·
FOUR THIRTY
SIXTH AVENUE
NEW · YORK · · · N·Y·

The Works Progress Administration (WPA) created by President Franklin D. Roosevelt in 1935 gave a large number of unemployed workers, including these men in Chicago, the opportunity to earn some money; it also helped many of them regain their self-respect after losing their jobs. Wright was assigned to several manual labor posts with the WPA before he joined the agency's Federal Writers' Project in 1935.

published book, *For My People*, won the Yale University Younger Poets Competition six years later. And he continued to work on his own writing.

In January, one of Wright's literary efforts paid off. His short story "Big Boy Leaves Home" was accepted for a prestigious anthology, *The New Caravan*, making it the first of his works to be available to a white mainstream audience. When the anthology appeared in November 1936, most of the book critics for the major newspapers and magazines, including the *New York Times* and *New Republic*, were unanimous in their praise and cited Wright's story as the finest piece in the collection.

"Big Boy Leaves Home," which was also published two years later in Wright's own story collection *Uncle Tom's Children: Four Novellas*, is set in the Mississippi of his childhood. The main character is a schoolboy who finds himself in the middle of a frightening, and ultimately deadly, racial encounter. Rather than become a victim he elects to assert himself—and therefore must leave the South.

By 1937, Wright could finally claim he was leading the life of a full-fledged writer. He was surrounded at the WPA as well as outside it by a lively group of people who were devoted to literature and the arts. Furthermore, his own writing was going well. His story "The Ethics of Living Jim Crow" was published in another anthology, *American Stuff*.

There was one drawback to Wright's way of life, however. More and more, he found it difficult to tolerate the demands of his fellow communists. Although he greatly admired the principles of equality they upheld, he was distressed by their desire to control him, especially at a time when he was more interested in his own projects than in working on reports and brochures and organizing activities for the party.

Wright's insistence on working on his own material, including *Lawd Today*, became a constant source of irritation to the party leaders, who felt he should be performing the tasks they requested. As in the past, he found himself at odds with those around him. "Racial hate had been the bane of my life," he said, "and here before my eyes was concrete proof that it could be abolished. Yet a new hate had come to take the place of the rankling racial hate. It was irrational that Communists should hate what they called 'intellectuals,' or anybody who tried to think for himself. I had fled men who did not like the color of my skin, and now I was among men who did not like the tone of my thoughts."

On May 1, Wright failed to march in the May Day Parade to help celebrate the annniversary of the Russian revolution. Communist officials in Chicago, uncertain of his loyalty to their party, had asked him not to take part in the march. Realizing that his relations with the party had cooled and the reactions of his reading audience were just warming up, Wright, at the age of 29, decided to leave Chicago, his home for a decade. The time had come for him to move to New York and make his way into the heart of the publishing world.

5

A WALL
OF FAME

Wright arrived in New York at the age of 28 and saw his literary fortunes rise immediately. In quick succession, he edited a quarterly magazine called New Challenge, *became the Harlem editor of the communist newspaper the* Daily Worker, *and won a nationwide literary contest.*

WEARING A BORROWED suit and lugging his typewriter, Wright hitched a ride to New York on the night of May 28, 1937. He arrived there the following day and spent his first few weeks in the city with an old friend, Abraham Chapman. After that, he rented a furnished room in a hotel on St. Nicholas Avenue in Harlem.

Wright's arrival coincided with the second American Writers' Congress, which he attended along with such well-known writers as Ernest Hemingway, Lillian Hellman, and Archibald MacLeish. At the conference, Wright publicly stressed the importance of holding one's own creative development above the political demands of the Communist party. His address did not please party officials. Nevertheless, they were so impressed by his literary gifts that they did not want to lose his services. This became clear two days later, when the editors of the *Daily Worker*, the Communist party newspaper, named the 28-year-old Wright as coeditor of a new literary quarterly, *New Challenge*.

Wright was happy to accept the post with *New Challenge*—even though he was still at odds with the party—because it put him in touch with some of the finest black writers of the day. For the journal's first issue, which was published in the fall of 1937, he collected numerous literary pieces, including articles by the poets Sterling Brown and Margaret Walker.

NEW CHALLENGE
A Literary Quarterly

VOLUME II   FALL 1937   NUMBER II

CONTENTS

EDITORS

DOROTHY WEST   MARIAN MINUS

ASSOCIATE EDITOR
RICHARD WRIGHT

CONTRIBUTING EDITORS: Sterling Brown, Collins George, Robert Hayden, Eugene Holmes, Langston Hughes, Russell Marshall, Loren Miller, Arthur Randall, Margaret Walker.

NEW CHALLENGE: Published quarterly, 25c a copy; $1.00 a year. Copyright 1937 by Dorothy West. No reprint may be made without permission of the editors. Make all checks payable to NEW CHALLENGE, 371 West 117th Street, N. Y. C.

In the spring of 1937, Wright was named editor of a new literary quarterly, New Challenge. This periodical enabled him to publish some of the nation's leading black writers.

He also accepted a review of Waters Edward Turpin's book *These Low Grounds* by an eager young writer named Ralph Ellison.

Ellison was a recent graduate of Tuskegee Institute, one the country's leading black institutions of higher learning, and he greatly admired Wright's poetry, especially his "I Have Seen Black Hands."

When he learned that a mutual friend, the poet Langston Hughes, knew Wright, he asked Hughes to arrange a meeting. Wright and Ellison soon became fast friends. In fact, after Wright read Ellison's book review, he encouraged Ellison to try his hand at writing a short story. The result, "Hymie's Bull," convinced Ellison to pursue a career as a writer, and he emerged as a leading literary figure in 1952, when he published one of the most powerful novels of the 20th century, *Invisible Man*.

Editing *New Challenge* was mainly a labor of love for Wright. The job paid very little and took up a great deal of his time and energy. Nevertheless, he managed to contribute an article of his own, called "Blueprint for Negro Literature," to the inaugural issue. This essay urged young black writers to stop imitating the works of white writers. Instead, Wright said, black writers should find the raw material for their subjects by mining their own rich racial heritage. In effect, "Blueprint for Negro Literature" was a call for black nationalism.

New Challenge turned out to be a short-lived venture. Nonetheless, Wright remained busy. Along with editing the journal, he had also been writing articles for the *Daily Worker*. As soon as *New Challenge* folded, he was named the *Daily Worker*'s Harlem bureau chief, a position that kept him in close touch with the Harlem community.

A shrewd and sympathetic observer, Wright favored news articles that showed the human as well as the political side of a story. It was typical of him to pen a piece entitled "Santa Claus Has a Hard Time Finding Way in Harlem Slums" after seeing a sign, hanging in a local office building, that read: MERRY CHRISTMAS—SPACE FOR RENT—WHITES ONLY. In addition to these articles, which included accounts of black heavyweight boxer Joe Louis's stirring victories to gain the world championship, he also reviewed books.

A close friendship between the author Ralph Ellison (shown here) and Wright blossomed in New York shortly after the 22-year-old Ellison read Wright's protest poems in leftist journals. "Indeed," Ellison said later, "such reading and wondering prepared me not only to meet Wright, but to seek him out."

Late at night, in the privacy of his tiny office at the *Daily Worker*, Wright managed to work on his own fiction as well. He was determined to enter several short stories—"Big Boy Leaves Home," "Down by the Riverside," "Long Black Song," and "Fire and Cloud"—in a national contest sponsored by *Story* magazine, and he worked feverishly to polish them before the deadline arrived. Once the stories were ready, he resigned from the *Daily Worker* and joined the WPA's Federal Writers' Project in New York, helping to research the New York section of the American Guidebook series. He left the *Daily Worker* largely because only writers employed by the WPA were eligible to take part in the contest.

In February 1938, the judges of the contest—the novelist Sinclair Lewis, the first American to win the Nobel Prize for literature; newspaper magnate Lewis Gannett; and Book-of-the-Month Club president Harry Scherman—chose "Fire and Cloud" as the best story out of 500 entries. "Wright's work stood head and shoulders above the rest," Gannett said in awarding him the first-prize money. According to Gannett, Wright's stories "sing as well as sear." The prize amounted to $500, a substantial amount during the Great Depression.

Happily, Wright told a reporter for the nation's leading black newspaper, the *Amsterdam News*, about his plans for the money. "I'm none of that school," he said, "that believes art thrives on empty stomachs and cold, dingy rooms." He spent part of his prize on an overcoat and a nice, juicy steak.

As word of Wright's prize-winning feat circulated around town, a variety of reactions followed. His friends showed little surprise, eager female fans sent him proposals of marriage, and several literary agents mailed him letters expressing their interest in representing him. Wright decided to talk further with Paul Reynolds, Jr., a well-known New York agent, who quickly signed the young writer to a contract with the Reynolds Literary Agency.

In the meantime, *Story* magazine was in the process of sending to a book publisher, Harper & Brothers, all four of the stories Wright had submitted to the contest. Harper agreed to publish the four pieces later in the year, under Wright's chosen title: *Uncle Tom's Children: Four Novellas*. In addition, Harper offered him a contract for a second work.

The tales in *Uncle Tom's Children* describe the terror that racism brings to the lives of Mississippi blacks. In each story, the main character experiences a traumatic event that takes him or her from childlike innocence to hardened militancy. All of the reviews of Wright's first book, which were uniformly positive, spoke of his mastery in capturing southern life.

"Although the talents of this young Negro have not gone unrecognized, *Uncle Tom's Children* will not only make the name familiar to all literate Americans but also startle those whose expectations have been high," Granville Hicks wrote in *New Masses*. "The U.S. has never had a first-rate Negro novelist. Last week the promise of one appeared," *Time* magazine reported. And the *New York World-Telegram* said, "In Mr. Wright the race has won a powerful champion."

With the publication of *Uncle Tom's Children*, Wright became a new literary star. Before long, his book was being read in high school and college classrooms around the country, and the national press of the U.S.S.R. was printing 75,000 copies of the book in Russian translation. Each day's mail brought him an invitation to lecture at a university, sign books at a store, or attend a charity ball. Chief among the more notable distinctions was a formal reception in New York's luxurious St. Moritz Hotel, where he was honored in November 1938 along with the writers Sherwood Anderson, Edgar Lee Masters, and Pearl Buck by the League of American Writers.

The novelist Sinclair Lewis was one of three judges who deemed Wright's short story "Fire and Cloud" the top entry in a nationwide contest sponsored by Story magazine. Shortly after winning first prize in the contest, Wright had his first book, Uncle Tom's Children, *published.*

By that time, Wright was immersed in another project: the story of Bigger Thomas and the sad effects of poverty and racism. "I found," he said of *Uncle Tom's Children*, "that I had written a book which even bankers' daughters could read and weep over and feel good about. I swore to myself that if ever I wrote another book, no one would weep over it; that it would be so hard and deep that they would have to face it without the consolation of tears."

Wright had since moved to Brooklyn, where he lived in an upstairs room in a two-family house belonging to his friends Jane and Herbert Newton, and he worked relentlessly on what would become his first published novel, *Native Son*. On some mornings, he tiptoed out of the house at 5:30 A.M. and walked over to Fort Greene Park, where he wrote for several hours atop a small hill, in the shadow of a revolutionary war monument. As soon as he knew Herbert was at work and the Newton children were either off to school or out at play, he returned to his room, completely absorbed in the plight of Bigger Thomas.

Wright also made a couple of trips to Chicago to verify the locale and details of his story. "Sometimes I worked so hard that my mind ceased to register and I had to take long walks," he said to Margaret Walker. "I had to get that book out and I wanted it out before the first one was forgotten."

To give himself more time to work on the novel, Wright applied for a Guggenheim Fellowship, a sizable artistic grant, knowing that if he received the award, he would be able to give up his post at the WPA. In May 1939, with the help of first lady Eleanor Roosevelt, who had read his work and had written a letter of recommendation to the Guggenheim board on his behalf, he was awarded a fellowship. Along with the writers John Steinbeck and Robert Penn Warren, he received a $2,500 stipend, which enabled him to quit the Federal Writers' Project and concentrate full-time on *Native Son*.

CALL *to the*
THIRD AMERICAN WRITERS CONGRESS

In the last two years, writers in other countries have sacrificed their lives and suffered exile and imprisonment. They have proved that the preservation of every form of culture is inseparable from the struggle of the people everywhere against those forces that seek the death of liberty in our time.

We can report that the League of American Writers, since its formation as a national organization at the congresses of 1935 and 1937, has increased its membership fourfold, and has worked actively in behalf of democratic culture wherever threatened. At the coming congress we will consider the media, markets, and associations by which we may increase the effectiveness of our professional aims. In particular we will consider the question of how mass audiences can most effectively be reached by existing media, such as motion pictures, radio and television.

The call to the Third American Writers Congress goes forth at a time when the world fears the outbreak of more invasions and wars. We address ourselves to all professional writers who recognize the need to face the immediate problems—technical, cultural, and political—that confront them today, and warmly invite them to attend.

We will discuss the following subjects, and shape a policy in relation to them:

The defense of democracy in the United States, cooperation of this country with other nations and peoples opposed to fascism — including the Soviet Union, which has been the most consistent defender of peace; cooperation with writers exiled from the fascist countries; support for the anti-fascist policies of the present administration; support for the labor unions; cooperation among all democratic and progressive forces; opposition to race prejudice; to attacks on social legislation and to efforts to cripple or abolish the Federal Arts Projects; in general, the defense of a free world in which writers can function.

We propose these subjects as a framework for discussion at the Congress, while welcoming further suggestions—if they are sent promptly. The Congress will be held in New York City, on June 2-3-4. Writers planning to attend it should get in touch with the Executive Secretary of the League of American Writers, 381 Fourth Avenue, New York, N. Y.

Benjamin Appel	Guy Endore	Meyer Levin	Vincent Sheean
Newton Arvin	Henry Pratt Fairchild	Helen Merrell Lynd	Viola Brothers Shore
Albert Bein	Francis Edward Faragoh	Albert Maltz	Upton Sinclair
Nora Benjamin	Kenneth Fearing	Bruce Minton	Tess Slesinger
Aline Bernstein	Arthur Davison Ficke	Ruth McKenney	Philip Stevenson
Millen Brand	Marjorie Fischer	Carey McWilliams	Donald Ogden Stewart
Bessie Breuer	Joseph Freeman	Harvey O'Connor	Irving Stone
Dorothy Brewster	Daniel Fuchs	Dorothy Parker	Leland Stowe
Louis Bromfield	Mauritz Hallgren	S. J. Perelman	Genevieve Taggard
Van Wyck Brooks	Henry Hart	Frederic Prokosch	James Thurber
Sidney Buchman	Lillian Hellman	Lorine Pruette	Frank Tuttle
Kenneth Burke	DuBose Heyward	Samuel Putnam	Jean Starr Untermeyer
Erskine Caldwell	Eugene Holmes	W. L. River	Louis Untermeyer
Katherine Garrison Chapin	Jess Kimbrough	Ralph Roeder	Carl Van Doren
Humphrey Cobb	Arthur Kober	Harold J. Rome	John Wexley
Lester Cohen	Alfred Kreymborg	Muriel Rukeyser	William Carlos Williams
Malcolm Cowley	Joshua Kunitz	Budd Wilson Schulberg	Ella Winter
George Dillon	David Lamson	Vida D. Scudder	Richard Wright
Muriel Draper	Jesse Lasky, Jr.	Edwin Seaver	Stanley Young
Philip Dunne	John Howard Lawson	Irwin Shaw	Leane Zugsmith

Wright was a featured speaker at the Third American Writers' Congress, held in June 1939 at the New School for Social Research in New York. Many of the nation's best-known writers— including Lillian Hellman and James Thurber—attended this biennial event, which was sponsored by the League of American Writers.

But there were some unexpected distractions. While working on his book one winter evening, he decided to take a break from his typewriter and go downstairs to the Newtons' living room, where a Communist party meeting was in progress. Among the participants was 26-year-old Ellen Poplar, a white and attractive Brooklyn native with green eyes and shining auburn curls. She was a local organizer for the party and extremely serious about her commitment to it.

During the course of subsequent party meetings, Wright became extremely attracted to Ellen and proposed marriage. She was cautious, however, about sealing their relationship. She knew that an interracial marriage could be difficult, and she was afraid that her parents and friends would cut her off if she accepted Wright's proposal. She left for a summer vacation without giving him an answer.

Ellen's failure to respond meant to Wright that she would reject his proposal. Accordingly, he began to spend his time with an old friend, Rose Dhimah Meadman, a stately ballet dancer of Russian extraction. He found this young divorcée, who had a two-year-old son, to be highly spirited and independent.

When Ellen returned from her vacation in early August, she rushed over to the Newtons' house to see Wright, anxious to let him know she had decided to marry him. She was met by the news that Wright had already made plans for his wedding—to Dhimah. The following week, Richard and Dhimah were married in the Episcopal church on Manhattan's Convent Avenue, with Ralph Ellison serving as best man.

In the months that followed, Wright readied *Native Son* for publication. The book was issued on March 1, 1940, and sold more than 200,000 copies within the first 3 weeks of publication. Some bookstores even sold out their copies in a matter of hours. The novel enabled him to become the first black American writer to reach a large mainstream audience.

Book critics everywhere began to compare Wright with such literary masters as Fyodor Dostoyevski, Theodore Dreiser, and Charles Dickens. Lewis Gannett said in the *New York Herald Tribune* that *Native Son* had "a depth and subtlety . . . which were not evident in 'Uncle Tom's Children,' and it is a far more harrowing story. [John Steinbeck's] 'Grapes of Wrath' is gentle by comparison." The *New York World-Telegram* said it was "a story that packs a tremendous punch, smashing like a big fist through the windows of our complacent lives. A story so horrible that it makes readers shudder, it also carries so much truth and justice in the telling that we read it to the end with . . . rapt attention."

RICHARD WRIGHT

NATIVE SON

With an Introduction "How 'Bigger' Was Born"
by the author

HARPER & ROW

ISBN 0-06-014762-8

Native Son

Richard Wright

From the beginning, Bigger was doomed. He was a "nigger" on Chicago's South Side, surrounded by rats and rebels with nowhere to go, a "nigger" in a white man's world. He might have been up for some petty crime, but by chance it was for murder and rape.

He killed the first girl in an unpremeditated moment of panic and was caught up by forces he could neither understand nor control. Murder led to a more brutal murder and Bigger at last felt alive: he had found in acts of violence the sense of manhood and freedom, distorted as they were, which Bessie, with her whiskey, and his mother, with her religion, had not been able to give him.

This classic novel is one of powerful

(Continued on back flap)

1169

"It's got to be good," Wright said of his first novel, Native Son, while preparing it for publication in March 1940, *"because I want to show that 'Uncle Tom's Children' was no accident."* Later editions of the novel included Wright's informative essay "How 'Bigger' Was Born."

Even the Book-of-the-Month Club, the nation's largest book club, responded favorably, choosing *Native Son* as one of two monthly selections to send to club members in March. It marked the first time ever that the club featured a novel by a black writer. Wright was worried, however, that the black press might not react as agreeably. After all, the book's hero, Bigger Thomas, was an antisocial character whose actions mirrored those of a trapped animal. He was not a model of which his race could be proud.

But Wright need not have feared. *"Native Son,"* the *Chicago Defender* reported, "shall not only focus attention upon the evils which are visited upon us, but . . . shall, by the very urgency of its message, transform a rotten social, economic system into a living democracy for all." James Ivy, a spokesman for the NAACP, wrote in *Crisis*, "It is a profound and searching analysis of the mind of the American Negro and a penetrating study of the tragic position of the Negro in American life."

The widespread critical acclaim turned Wright into a highly sought after public figure. Sacks of fan

Wright became widely regarded as America's leading black author upon the publication of Native Son. *"In this country there were good Negro writers before Wright arrived on the scene," Ralph Ellison said, "but it seems to me that Richard Wright wanted more and dared more. . . . He wanted to be tested in terms of his talent, and not in terms of his race."*

mail arrived daily at his doorstep. He was besieged with requests to write articles and reviews and became a favorite subject for magazine and newspaper interviews (some journalists reported on his charm and openness; others said he was arrogant and reserved). His name was inscribed on a Wall of Fame along with other distinguished Americans at the New York World's Fair, which opened in 1939 and continued through 1940.

The constant whirlwind of publicity prompted Wright to consider taking a vacation for the first time in his life. He discussed the idea with Dhimah, and they decided to go to Mexico. She enthusiastically made arrangements to transport not only her husband, herself, and her young son but also her mother, her piano, and the pianist who accompanied her daily dance rehearsals.

Once in Cuernavaca, Mexico, Wright found it impossible to do any work on a new novel he was calling *Little Sister* (in fact, it has yet to be published). Encouraged by Dhimah, old friends from New York as well as new friends from the local aristocracy kept a constant party going at the Wrights' rented villa. As much as Richard longed for peaceful solitude, Dhimah liked to be in the limelight.

In July 1940, an annoyed Wright left Dhimah in Mexico and journeyed across the South to Chapel Hill, North Carolina, to work with the playwright Paul Green on a stage adaptation of *Native Son*. On the way, he had a hurried reunion in Natchez with his father. He then spent the next month and a half working with Green. John Houseman, the producer of the play, drove down to North Carolina from New York to help smooth out some rough edges in the production, then drove Wright back north in September.

By that time, Dhimah had also made her way to New York. As soon as both of them were resettled in Brooklyn, divorce proceedings began. ❧

6

THESE
TROUBLED
DAYS

———————— ❧ ————————

W RIGHT MOVED BACK to the Newtons' house in Brooklyn as soon as his marriage to Dhimah came to an end. His friends still hosted weekly Communist party meetings in their living room, which Ellen Poplar continued to attend. At the first party meeting following Wright's return, he and Ellen took one look at each other and literally collapsed into each other's arms. They set a wedding date for March 12 of the coming year, after which they planned on moving into a small Harlem apartment on 140th Street, near where Ralph Ellison lived.

An unexpected yet welcome celebration preceded their wedding ceremony. In January 1941, Wright was awarded the highest honor bestowed on black Americans, the NAACP's Spingarn Medal for distinguished achievement. The judging committee voted him the award for what it called "his powerful depiction, in his works *Uncle Tom's Children* and *Native Son*, of the effects of discrimination and segregation and the denial of his rights as a citizen on the American Negro."

Wright drafted an eloquent acceptance speech he planned to deliver at the annual NAACP meeting. It addressed the burning topic of the day—the possibility of a second world war—and stressed that blacks should not let an impending war distract them from their struggle against racial prejudice in Amer-

Wright with bandleader Count Basie at a studio session late in 1940. The two men collaborated on a song called "King Joe (Joe Louis Blues)"—Wright penned the lyrics and Basie composed the music—that was eventually recorded by the noted singer and actor Paul Robeson.

73

ica. "We shall fight as determinedly against those who deny freedom at home," he wrote, "as we shall fight against those who deny it to others abroad."

Communist party leaders thought the tone of Wright's address made him out to be too much of a pacifist and ordered him to rework his speech. Their demand humiliated the 32-year-old writer, who felt his hard-won position as a spokesman for the black community was being ignored by the Communist party. Furthermore, he did not like the idea of having others temper his statements. He had disliked it when he was a junior high school student preparing a valedictory address, and now he liked it even less.

Nevertheless, Wright acquiesced to the party. At the awards ceremony in Houston, he bowed his head when the time came for the medal to be placed around his neck. "I accept this," he told the audience in a solemn voice, "in the name of the stalwart, enduring Negroes whose fate and destiny I have sought to depict . . . for they are my people, and my writing—which is my life and which carries my convictions—attempts to mirror their struggle for freedom during these troubled days." The episode further alienated him from the Communist party, however.

When Wright returned to New York, rehearsals for the stage production of *Native Son* were ready to begin. Less than a month later, just as the final run-throughs were being staged, he and Ellen were married. They had already agreed to postpone their honeymoon because the play was scheduled to open on Broadway in two weeks.

The premiere of *Native Son* and its subsequent reviews aroused a great deal of popular interest. After 114 performances at the St. James Theatre on Broadway, the show moved uptown, to the Apollo Theater in Harlem, and then on to the Maplewood Theatre in the Bronx. At this last stop in New York, it broke the theater's all-time attendance record.

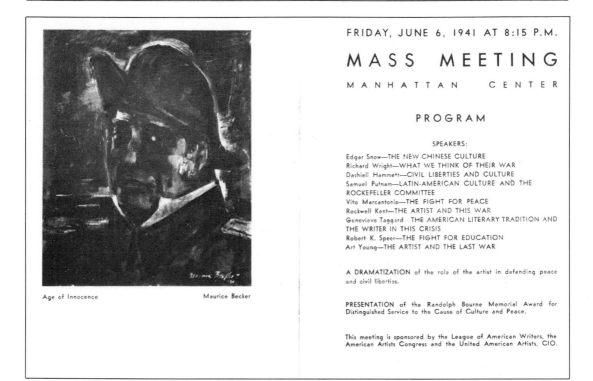

Age of Innocence   Maurice Becker

FRIDAY, JUNE 6, 1941 AT 8:15 P.M.

MASS MEETING

MANHATTAN   CENTER

PROGRAM

SPEAKERS:

Edgar Snow—THE NEW CHINESE CULTURE
Richard Wright—WHAT WE THINK OF THEIR WAR
Dashiell Hammett—CIVIL LIBERTIES AND CULTURE
Samuel Putnam—LATIN-AMERICAN CULTURE AND THE
ROCKEFELLER COMMITTEE
Vito Marcantonio—THE FIGHT FOR PEACE
Rockwell Kent—THE ARTIST AND THIS WAR
Genevieve Taggard THE AMERICAN LITERARY TRADITION AND
THE WRITER IN THIS CRISIS
Robert K. Speer—THE FIGHT FOR EDUCATION
Art Young—THE ARTIST AND THE LAST WAR

A DRAMATIZATION of the role of the artist in defending peace
and civil liberties.

PRESENTATION of the Randolph Bourne Memorial Award for
Distinguished Service to the Cause of Culture and Peace.

This meeting is sponsored by the League of American Writers, the
American Artists Congress and the United American Artists, CIO.

When *Native Son* left the city to play in theaters across the country, its powerful antiracist message often met with resistance. Armed policemen patrolled the lobby of Baltimore's Ford Theatre to prevent the posting of any photographs that showed black and white actors in the same scene and to make sure that blacks did not enter the orchestra seats. Such measures, however, did not stop Wright's play from inspiring the theatergoers. *Native Son* often drew shouts of affirmation and approval from the audience, especially in the South. "You can't imagine what it means to say what you've always wanted to say and to say it precisely to the people it was meant for," one of the actors remarked to a theater critic.

While the play toured the country, Wright mapped out a 150-page book, first writing out the manuscript on long sheets of yellow paper and then revising it a half-dozen times on his typewriter. He

Wright maintained his ties with the League of American Writers even though his relationship with the Communist party deteriorated in the early 1940s. He is listed as a featured speaker in this program from the Fourth American Writers' Congress.

titled this work of nonfiction *Twelve Million Black Voices: A Folk History of the Negro in the United States* because his narrative, which often used the first-person plural *we*, claimed to speak for all black Americans. Combining a straightforward text with pictures taken by the Photographic Section of the WPA's Farm Security Administration and edited by Edwin Rosskam, the book was published in November 1941, and the reviews it received were nothing short of remarkable.

"The text is far from commonplace," the *New York World-Telegram* said. "Indeed, the name of Richard Wright guarantees sincerity, earnestness and a degree of power." The New York *Sunday Worker* reported, "It is perhaps the first realistic, class-conscious narrative of the Negro people in the United States ever to be gotten together." And the *New York Times* added, "A more eloquent statement of its kind could hardly have been devised."

Wright begins *Twelve Million Black Voices* by looking back at slavery and the rural South in an attempt to explain the rise of the urban black ghettos. He then discusses the period from the Civil War until World War I and concludes the book with a current view of black life in the United States. For this last section, he stopped at local hangouts—parks and soda shops—and interviewed the people there. "Look at us and know us," Wright tells the reader, "and you will know yourselves, for *we* are *you*, looking back at you from the dark mirror of our lives."

While working on *Twelve Million Black Voices,* Wright settled into married life and a peaceful domestic routine. He learned about photography, cooked elaborate meals with Ellen, and designed furniture for their home. Before long, Ellen, who had seen her family ties with the Poplars unravel because her relatives objected to an interracial marriage, hap-

Wright's haunting illustrated folk history, Twelve Million Black Voices, *was published in November 1941, a year and a half after* Native Son, *and immediately established him as an important writer of nonfiction. In it he wrote of his fellow blacks, "Even though we have been told that we need not be afraid, we have lived so long in fear of all white faces that we cannot help but sit and wait."*

pily announced to her husband that they were about to start a family of their own.

On April 15, 1942, Wright peered through the window of a hospital delivery room and saw his daughter, Julia, for the first time. Apparently, the presence of a granddaughter softened the hearts of the Poplar family. Ellen and her parents patched up their differences shortly after Julia's birth.

It seemed, at least on the surface, that life could hardly be better for Wright. He had a happy family and a successful career—the very things he had longed for during his youth. Below the surface, however, the course of his life was quietly being undermined by the U.S. government. Although he had absolutely no knowledge of it, the publication of *Twelve Million Black Voices* had sealed his reputation as a dangerous subversive.

In 1938, the U.S. House of Representatives had created the House Un-American Activities Committee (HUAC) to look into the affairs of U.S. citizens whom the government suspected of acting against American interests. The committee was supposed to curtail the steady flow of communist propaganda that was heightening the nation's fear of communism and the Soviet Union, which was on the rise as an international power. But by the early 1940s, the committee was doing more than just stopping the propaganda issued by left-wing organizations. Many liberal-minded individuals whom HUAC regarded as subversive were placed under investigation. The Federal Bureau of Investigation (FBI) worked closely with the committee during this period.

After *Twelve Million Black Voices* was published, the FBI received a letter requesting that charges be brought "against one Richard Wright, author of *Native Son, Twelve Million Black Voices* and other vile publications" and calling for "the arrest of Wright and confiscation of every copy of his books." Another letter, sent to Secretary of War Henry Stimson and forwarded to J. Edgar Hoover, director of the FBI, cautioned that Wright's latest book was "designed to destroy the morale of American citizens . . . and corrupt national unity."

On December 1, 1942, Hoover issued a firm directive to the FBI's New York field office. An agent there was to scrutinize all of Wright's works for un-American themes. "And if your inquiry develops information of an affirmative nature," the agent was

Shortly after Twelve Million Black Voices *was published, J. Edgar Hoover, director of the Federal Bureau of Investigation (FBI), the investigative and law enforcement branch of the U.S. Department of Justice, ordered his staff to inquire into Wright's daily affairs. For the rest of his life, Wright was kept under surveillance by the FBI.*

told, "you should of course cause an investigation to be undertaken as to subject's background, inclinations, and current activities."

Ironically, just as Wright was being investigated as a subversive by the FBI, his association with the Communist party was drawing to a close. In the summer of 1942, he officially withdrew from the party's roster. "When I was a member of the Communist Party, I took that party seriously, and when I discovered that I was holding a tainted instrument in my hands, I dropped that instrument," he wrote to his editor and friend Edward Aswell.

Wright attempted to explain his actions to the world at large in "I Tried to Be a Communist," a two-part article that appeared in *Atlantic Monthly* in 1943. "I wanted to be a Communist, but my kind of Communist," he wrote in the essay, which gave a detailed account of the injustices he suffered under the party leaders. Nevertheless, leaving the party left him in an unenviable position. "When I left the Communist Party," he wrote to Aswell, "I no longer had a protective barrier, no defenses between me and a hostile racial environment that absorbed all of my time, emotions, and attention. To me the racial situation was a far harder matter than the Communist one and it was one that I could not solve alone."

The "racial situation" heated up in the United States during World War II as the federal government supported several discriminatory measures and chose to ignore the issue of prejudice. Blacks were denied jobs at defense industry plants and were permitted to serve only in segregated units in the army, where they had little chance of becoming officers. Another insulting policy prevented black soldiers from donating blood to army hospitals. Eventually, a public outcry prompted the army to change this restriction, thereby enabling blacks to give blood. Their plasma was not administered to white patients, however.

Black grievances came to a head during the middle of 1943. In June, 34 people were killed and many more were injured in a violent race riot that broke out in Detroit. A little over a month later, Harlem became the scene of widespread fury. The wounding of a black soldier by a white policeman initiated a night of mob violence that saw blacks battle in the streets with police and national guardsmen. Five blacks were killed, and many more were injured.

Wright visited the devastated streets of Harlem shortly after the riot took place. Many of the white-owned stores that had not employed black workers had been looted and burned. Newscasters at the scene heard Wright say the rioting had been triggered by deeply rooted feelings of anger and resentment known only to the poor, and he pleaded for a financial aid program to help the poverty-stricken ghetto.

Looters being escorted from the New York City district of Harlem in August 1943 after a night of widespread rioting left the black ghetto totally devastated. One month later, Wright organized a citizens' committee to examine many of the community's racial problems.

Images of a devastated Harlem burned in Wright's mind for weeks, and they ultimately moved him to take further action. In September, he organized the Citizens' Emergency Conference for Interracial Unity. The members of this group studied the daily lives and problems of Harlem residents and worked to find solutions to the community's sense of unrest.

By this time, Wright had moved with his family to the ground floor of a large Victorian house at 7 Middagh Street in Brooklyn Heights, near the Brooklyn Bridge. This building was also the home of the writer Carson McCullers, and it served as a meeting place for a number of prominent people, including the painter Salvador Dali, the composer and critic Virgil Thomson, and the singer Lotte Lenya. After a year in this raucous household, Wright decided to

"I used to brood upon the unconscious irony of those who felt that Negroes led so passional an existence!" Wright said. "I saw that what had been taken for our emotional strength was our negative confusions, our flights, our fears, our frenzy under pressure."

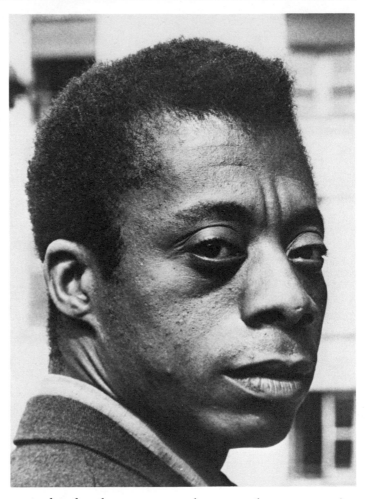

Novelist and essayist James Baldwin received some welcome assistance from Wright shortly after they met for the first time early in 1945. Nevertheless, their friendship soured four years later, when Baldwin attacked Wright's work in an article entitled "Everybody's Protest Novel."

move his family to a quieter home in the same neighborhood.

Because Wright was the sole supporter of his family, he was exempt from the military draft. When he tried to enlist, he failed to pass the army's battery of admission tests. Nevertheless, he volunteered for the army's press relations outfit in New York, putting together a massive publicity campaign that used posters, articles, songs, and radio announcements aimed at the black population. He asked to be officially recruited into the radio section of the armed forces, and he even traveled to the nation's capital to fill out the necessary forms. He was never accepted into military service, however, perhaps because he was a known communist sympathizer and had repeatedly spoken out against the government's racial policies.

Instead, Wright spent the war years at home, often helping out his fellow writers, particularly those who were young and promising. He read Henrietta Buckmaster's *Let My People Go*, a manuscript about the Underground Railroad and the hundreds of fugitive slaves who escaped to freedom in the North, and wrote a glowing description of the work, which her publishers used on the book's cover for promotional purposes. He was quick to recommend the novelist Nelson Algren's *Never Come Morning* to his own publisher and lobbied for the writer Laurence Lipton, who was working on a novel entitled *Brother the Laugh Is Bitter*, to receive a Guggenheim Fellowship.

Most notably of all, Wright helped an aspiring young black writer named James Baldwin, who was in desperate need of financial assistance. Thanks to Wright, Baldwin received the Eugene F. Saxton Memorial Trust Award, a grant that eased his pursuit of what turned out to be a brilliant literary career. In the years that followed, a warm relationship developed between the two writers, and Wright often came to Baldwin's aid when he needed money. Yet this financial arrangement, along with Baldwin's public criticism of Wright's work, ultimately damaged their friendship.

It was one of several associations Wright saw come to an end in the ensuing years. ❧

7
AN UNFINISHED TASK

❧

IN APRIL 1943, one of the largest black colleges in the South, Fisk University in Nashville, Tennessee, asked Wright to lecture there. The university also invited his friend and fellow writer Horace Cayton, who subsequently collaborated with the anthropologist and educator St. Clair Drake on *Black Metropolis: A Study of Negro Life in a Northern City*, a book along the lines of *Twelve Million Voices*. Wright went to Chicago to meet with Cayton, and from there the two men traveled to Tennessee. Not fond of flying, Wright convinced Cayton, that they should travel by train and use the time on board to write their lectures. Wright planned to speak simply and honestly about his experiences with racial prejudice and about his life as a young boy growing up in the South.

The train trip reacquainted Wright with the humiliation of racial segregation. In the dining car, he and Cayton were asked to stand in line and wait until all of the white diners had been seated. When their turn finally came, they were motioned to a table near the noisy pantry, where the waiters filled the coffeepots and cleaned the trays. This was the lone section

Wright at age 36, just after Black Boy *was published. "I have always taken the writing of literature very seriously," he said, "and I've looked upon fiction and writing in general as a means of revealing the truth of life and experience rather than purely as a means of entertaining people."*

of the car reserved for blacks. As soon as they were seated, a waiter bustled over to their table and pulled a curtain around them, hiding them from the view of the white diners.

By the time the train reached Nashville, Wright had plenty of material for his lecture. Just before he began his address, he stood at the podium and gazed at the large crowd of black and white faces, a rare mix for the South. The topic of his speech was the fear and hunger he had known as a young black southerner.

Wright heard faint applause and a few nervous giggles as his address drew to a close. "I had accidentally blundered into the secret, black, hidden core of race relations in the United States," he said later. "That core is: nobody is expected to speak honestly about the problem . . . everybody is expected in polite society to wrap the problem up in myth, legend, morality, folklore, niceties, and just plain lies."

But much to Wright's surprise, students and faculty members made their way over to him later on in the evening and thanked him for breaking the code of silence on racial prejudice. "Goddam," one professor told him, "you're the first man to tell the truth in this town." The overwhelming response of his audience, so hesitant and fearful at first, made Wright resolve that night to begin work on an autobiography. He was determined to make white Americans understand the black world they refused to acknowledge, and the first step was to show them the reality of it.

Although the 34-year-old Wright was widely known as a writer, his childhood experiences had been the same as those of thousands of poor southern blacks. "One of the things that made me write," he said, "is that I realize that I'm a very average Negro. . . . Maybe that's what makes me extraordinary."

By December, Wright had completed the soul-searching process of writing his autobiography and had sent the manuscript off to his agent, Paul Reynolds. The text spanned his entire life, from childhood to the present. Yet his agent and his publisher felt it best to separate his early experiences from his adult ones. Wright agreed to their suggestion and reworked the manuscript.

The result was *Black Boy: A Record of Childhood and Youth*. The book chronicles Wright's life from his birth in the Mississippi delta to his flight to Chicago at age 17. The later years of his life, including his ups and downs with the Communist party and his move to New York, were described in the essay "I Tried to Be a Communist" as well as in the book *American Hunger*, which was published posthumously in 1977.

The prospect of continuing royalty payments from *Black Boy* enabled the Wrights to look into buying a house in New England. They saw one in Vermont and were anxious to purchase it, but the owner refused to sell it to them because Wright was black. Even-

None of Wright's books were more popular or created more of a sensation than Black Boy, *a largely autobiographical account of his childhood and youth. Issued in February 1945, it was the last of his books to be published while he was living in the United States.*

tually, they decided to remain in New York, moving into a house on Charles Street in Greenwich Village, the city's artistic and intellectual center, in February 1945.

Black Boy sent shock waves around the country when it hit the bookstores that same month. Some readers were alarmed by the bleak picture it painted; others were upset by the book's rough language. But most readers were deeply affected by Wright's characterization of black life in the South. In fact, for many of them, his words allowed them to enter this realm for the very first time. "It is powerful, moving and horrifying," the *New York Times* said of the book.

Like *Native Son*, *Black Boy* became a Book-of-the-Month Club main selection and reigned on the best-seller lists for nearly a year, reaching the top spot in April and remaining there through June. Within three months of its publication, the book's sales climbed to more than half a million copies. Foreign rights were sold to England, Brazil, Palestine, Argentina, and Scandinavia. Late in the year, it received five votes from the Pulitzer Prize committee, barely losing out to Arthur Schlesinger, Jr.'s *The Age of Jackson*, which won the prize with six votes.

Still, *Black Boy* had its detractors, including the critic Ben Burns of the *Chicago Defender*, who called the work "a sorry slander of the Negro." In addition to hundreds of fan letters, Wright received vicious messages informing him that the South had no intention of ever changing. One bookstore in Nashville flatly refused to stock any copies of the autobiography, and in Deming, New Mexico, the commander of the air force base there banned the book from its library.

Black Boy was even discussed on the Senate floor. On June 25, Senator Theodore Bilbo of Mississippi referred to Wright's scathing depiction of racism during the politician's attempts to forestall an integration measure. "The purpose of the book," the senator said, "is to plant the seeds of hate in every Negro in America against the white men of the South or against the white race anywhere, for that matter. . . . It is the dirtiest, filthiest, lousiest, most obscene piece of writing that I have ever seen in print. . . . But it comes from a Negro and you cannot expect any better from a person of this type."

Wright took advantage of the controversy to get his message heard. Whenever he was interviewed, he spoke against the evils of racism. Often, he pleaded for blacks to recognize their contribution to American culture and to embrace their heritage proudly. He appeared at the annual meeting of the National

"I feel that literature ought to be a sharp instrument to reveal something important about mankind, about living, about life whether among whites or blacks," Wright said. *"That is why my work hews so close to facts, and yet why I try to float these facts on a sea of emotion."*

Sharecroppers' Union to deliver a speech entitled "What Peace Will Bring to the South" and often lectured on behalf of the NAACP. He envisioned a nation, he said, "where there will exist no residential segregation, no Jim Crow army, no Jim Crow navy, no Jim Crow Red Cross Blood Bank, no Negro institutions, no laws prohibiting intermarriage, no customs assigning Negroes to inferior positions. We would simply be Americans and the nation would be better for it."

In October, Wright set out on an extensive lecture tour, winding his way across the country from campus to campus. Standing before teachers' associations, student assemblies, and political organizations, he attacked the harmful stereotype of blacks that abounded in literature. He urged university students to go out and complete what he called the "unfinished task of democracy" by treating every citizen with respect.

The hectic pace of this tour quickly sapped Wright's strength. He was originally scheduled to deliver 50 lectures but was able to complete only 14 of them. He became so mentally and physically exhausted that the rest of the speaking engagements were canceled.

In March 1946, Wright spent much of his time working on a cherished project with his friend Dr. Frederick Wertham, a psychiatrist and author of *Dark Legend*, a book that explores the motives of a man who murders his mother and contains many insights into pathological behavior and social conditioning. Wertham was also director of the mental health clinic of Queens General Hospital, where he cared for many of the area's juvenile delinquents. He believed there was an urgent need for a similar type of clinic in Harlem, and Wright volunteered to help set it up.

The 37-year-old writer called on a number of foundations and public organizations to finance a free

Wright's second wife, the former Ellen Poplar.

psychiatric clinic. But the responses left him sorely disappointed. No one was willing to risk the anger of the medical community by making free health care available.

Wright in turn wrote two articles, "Psychiatry Comes to Harlem" and "Juvenile Delinquency in Harlem," in which he criticized the people in the medical profession for their lack of social conscience. Thanks to his essays, several doctors and social workers volunteered their services and, without a penny of outside financial support, founded the Lafargue Clinic in the basement of St. Philip's Church in Harlem. From the moment the clinic opened its doors—on April 8, 1946—its rooms were filled with the delinquents and the troubled poor who came to receive counseling either for a 25-cent donation or, more often than not, for free. By February of the following year, the Lafargue Clinic had become such

Wright's last home in the United States was in New York's Greenwich Village. Although the neighborhood was known as a bohemian center for writers and artists, he was not accepted by the local community because he was black.

a respected mental health center that General Omar Bradley, the director of the Veterans Administration, assigned to it the care of all war veterans in New York, regardless of race.

Wright was not fooled by such triumphs. As the days passed, he became less and less hopeful of seeing racial prejudice come to an end in America. He was known the world over as an important black writer, yet he had to go all the way from his primarily white neighborhood to the black district of Harlem if he wanted to get his hair cut. He was considered an international authority on race relations, but he might still be served "salted coffee," a popular trick in restaurants to harass black customers. He had recently been stopped in front of the elevators in a hotel lobby on his way to a lunch appointment with Sinclair Lewis and was directed to take the service staircase instead. And his ownership of a house on Charles Street, which he was able to buy only by keeping his color a secret and dealing through a white lawyer, was a constant irritation to his new neighbors. When their barrage of insults and petitions failed to oust him, the neighbors went so far as to offer the Wrights $20,000 for the house into which they had just moved.

Most alarming of all were the increasing outbreaks of violence that Wright witnessed. Bands of young white men took to "patrolling" Greenwich Village, heaving blacks out of stores and attacking interracial couples. "To be in Washington Park during the forties," a black poet wrote at the time, "was to take your life in your hands. To be with a white woman was to commit suicide."

It was readily apparent to Wright that the color of his skin would always keep him from being accepted by white society. No matter how much he wrote or lectured, he would never be able to make enough of a difference to bring about racial equality in America. That job, he said, "is too big and life is too short."

As the spring of 1946 wore on, Wright gave serious thought to leaving the United States. He had tried living in various parts of the country—the South, the Midwest, the East—without ever feeling truly at home. Perhaps, he realized, it was best to move out of the country altogether. ❧

8

"I CHOOSE
EXILE"

***

WRIGHT'S FIRST TRIP overseas was abetted by the French government, which invited him on a monthlong, all-expenses-paid visit to the city of Paris. After encountering some difficulty in obtaining his passport because of his affiliation with the Communist party, he boarded the *Brazil* with his wife and daughter on May 1, 1946, and sailed across the Atlantic to Le Havre, in northern France. Unlike his boat ride up the Mississippi more than 30 years earlier, he traveled in style and comfort.

Once Wright made his way to Paris, he felt even more at ease. From his very first moments in the French capital—when friend and fellow writer Gertrude Stein arranged for a limousine to transport his travel-worn family through the city—he was treated like a celebrity and was made to feel wanted. Race never seemed to be an issue. "I could live and die in Paris!" he exclaimed.

Wright visited several other European countries in 1946. France's bohemian City of Lights had won his heart, however. "There is more freedom in one square block of Paris," he later wrote (in an essay entitled "I Choose Exile"), "than in the entire United States."

Wright stopped off in London before returning to New York in January 1947. There he met the writer George Padmore, a West Indian who was assisting the African colonies in gaining their independence

Wright at his desk in Paris. Although his best-known works were written in the United States, the majority of his books were published during the years that he lived abroad.

from Europe's imperial powers, especially the British, the French, and the Dutch. Padmore introduced Wright to a political and social movement known as Pan-Africanism, which promoted African customs and values and was looking to foster a huge Pan-African nation. Like communism and black nationalism, Pan-Africanism focused on helping a multitude of oppressed people, and the movement caught Wright's interest.

Wright became more deeply involved in Pan-Africanism the following August, when he and his family left New York on the *Queen Elizabeth* and moved permanently to France. In Paris, he formed close ties with the Présence Africaine, a group of African writers and activists who were in close contact with Padmore. Wright helped the members of this political circle publish a magazine, *Présence Africaine*, to air their views. Many of France's most prominent intellectuals, such as the philosopher Jean-Paul Sartre and the writers Albert Camus and André Gide, supported the venture.

In May 1948, Wright and his family settled into an apartment on rue Monsieur le Prince in Paris's

Paris served as Wright's home base while he was in self-imposed exile. "Yet, exile though I am," he said, "I remain unalterably and simply American."

Latin Quarter, an area that resembled Greenwich Village in artistic temperament. Wright kept himself busy with a variety of projects. In addition to publishing *Présence Africaine*, he started to write another novel, *The Outsider*. He also lectured all over France, worked closely with the French-American Fellowship (an organization that fought job discrimination in certain American businesses based in Europe), and enlarged his family's new home. On January 17, 1949, the added space was put to excellent use when the Wrights' second daughter, Rachel, was born.

Wright, at age 42, portrayed the teenaged Bigger Thomas in the 1951 film version of Native Son. *He purposely lost a great deal of weight to make himself look younger for the part.*

By summertime, Wright was caught up in yet another project: the film version of *Native Son*. He and the French director Pierre Chenal left Paris in August to work on the movie. They traveled first to New York, where they wrote the script and cast most of the characters, and proceeded on to Chicago, Haiti, and Argentina for the filming.

Unfortunately for Wright, the making of *Native Son* did not go very smoothly. The director, Chenal, fell behind schedule, and the producer, James Prades, ran into trouble with the film's backers. Both Chenal and Prades left the project during the middle of the shooting.

Eventually, the movie was put completely in Wright's hands. The 40-year-old writer became the film's producer and director. He also helped edit and arrange distribution of the picture. All told, the entire project took up almost a year and a half of his time.

Not surprisingly, Wright encountered many other difficulties, and they ultimately undermined the production. Although *Native Son* was fairly well received during its previews in Argentina, American audiences greeted the motion picture with a chorus of boos. Most film critics did not like the movie either; the *New York Times* called it "awkwardly amateurish." Wright's American distributor did not make things any easier by cutting several key scenes from the

Newspaper advertisements for the film Native Son *featured a still of Wright as Bigger Thomas carrying the body of Mary Dalton (played by Jean Wallace) along with the headline "The Dynamite Loaded Story of a Negro and a White Girl!" "I offer no alibis for this picture," Wright said of the movie. "Good or bad, it's what I wanted."*

movie, including the opening frames, in which Bigger Thomas savagely kills a rat.

Another major problem with *Native Son* was its hodgepodge cast: an ensemble of multilingual, international actors who did not mesh well with one another. Most notably miscast was the leading man. Wright himself played the part of the teenaged Bigger Thomas, even though he was busily filling the roles of producer and director and was at least 20 years too old for the main part. His inexperience as an actor did not help matters.

In late 1950, while Wright was making *Native Son* in Chicago, he agreed to write a series of articles for editor Ben Burns at *Ebony* magazine. But when Wright submitted the first of his pieces, "I Choose Exile," the magazine refused to publish it. The essay, which contained his complaints about American society and openly discussed his reasons for leaving the country, was in direct conflict with a nationwide campaign led by Senator Joseph McCarthy, who had managed to turn the HUAC investigations into a ruthless hunt for traitors, subversives, and spies. It was not the right time to publish someone who did not have positive things to say about the United States.

To Wright, the situation was familiar ground: His opinions were again being viewed as dangerous. Yet he refused to be silenced. He grappled with the way blacks and other minorities were treated by the Western world and dealt with this topic in *The Outsider*, his second novel. This book, which was published in March 1953, managed to blend the subject of race into a study of modern-day alienation.

Deeply philosophical, *The Outsider* is a far different kind of book from Wright's first novel, *Native Son*, which was written in a highly naturalistic style. Moreover, the main character, Cross Damon, is very different from Bigger Thomas, even though both men commit acts of violence. Whereas the illiterate Bigger is a victim of his environment, Damon is an astute black man in search of the meaning of existence.

Unlike Wright's earlier books, *The Outsider* did not prove to be a complete critical success. The *Washington Post* said, "It exasperates and abrades— but . . . it may be for its readers nearly as important a book as it was for its author." Granville Hicks in the *New York Times Book Review* likened the novel to Ralph Ellison's recently published *Invisible Man*, adding that Wright's book "is easy to disagree with, impossible to disregard." Other reviewers felt that Wright himself had become too much of an outsider; he had lived too long outside the United States to write convincingly about it.

After Wright completed this novel on alienation, he decided to realize a long-held dream and visit Africa. He was anxious to observe the ways in which black Africans were making the transition from a tribal civilization to an increasingly industrial one, and he was looking forward to describing what he saw to his readers. In preparation for his trip, he spent several months reading up on the history of Africa and European colonialism.

Wright was officially invited to visit the Gold Coast (which later became Ghana) by Kwame Nkrumah, the prime minister of the West African colony. The two men had become acquainted years earlier in

In 1953, 13 years after the appearance of Native Son, *Wright published his second novel,* The Outsider. *Wright's sense of being an outcast was underscored not only by the book's title but by its dedication, which read: "For Rachel, my daughter who was born on alien soil."*

An American Negro
views the African Gold Coast

BLACK
POWER

RICHARD WRIGHT

by the author of
NATIVE SON and BLACK BOY

"I was black and they were black, but my blackness did not help me," Wright wrote in Black Power: A Record of Reactions in a Land of Pathos, *a chronicle of his experiences in Africa. Yet he understood that he was bound to all Africans: "In terms of a common heritage of suffering and hunger for freedom,"* he said, *"your heart and my heart beat as one."*

the United States. Helping to arrange Wright's trip was George Padmore, who had been appointed Nkrumah's political adviser.

Wright set sail aboard a huge cruise ship early in June 1953. When he arrived in the Gold Coast, he was surprised by what he saw: a primitive people living in what he called "indescribably African confusion." Traveling by day under a merciless sun, he wandered through the cities, villages, and jungles of the region, scribbling hundreds of pages of notes and taking countless photographs of everything from the alleyways of Jamestown to the fishing villages of Labadi.

Wright's observations were published in September 1954 under the title *Black Power: A Record of Reactions in a Land of Pathos*. Walter White, the executive secretary of the NAACP, called this book "the most up to date, hopeful and valuable picture yet written of the most important experiment in democratic living." Wright's journalistic abilities were hailed as first-class and spurred his publisher to offer him a contract for another nonfiction book, *The Color Curtain: A Report on the Bandung Conference*, which was issued a year and a half later.

Wright's third novel, *Savage Holiday*, which was also published in 1954, did not receive the same kind of attention as *Black Power*. This psychological study of a white insurance man named Erskine Fowler was rejected by both his agent and his publisher before it was picked up by a paperback house. The American press, which deemed it a minor potboiler and quite atypical of Wright's work, declined to review it.

In 1954, Wright also began work on a book about Spain. Fortified by a $500 advance from his publisher, he traveled from Paris to Barcelona, where he moved into the home of a middle-class family and closely observed what their daily life was like. He remained in Spain from August to December, touring Madrid, Seville, and Granada, and returned for a second visit that took him into the Basque provinces in February 1955, the same month that he bought a farmhouse in Normandy.

Two months later, Wright took a break from his book on Spain and went to Bandung, Indonesia, to attend a conference held by the representatives of 29 newly independent but underdeveloped Third World nations. All of the African and Asian delegates at this conference voiced their displeasure with colonial rule and their support for racial equality. Wright's report on the Bandung Conference, which he called "the last call of westernized Asians to the moral conscience of the West," was published in March 1956 as *The Color Curtain: A Report on the Bandung Conference*.

That same year, Wright started sorting out the notes he had taken in Spain during hundreds of conversations with people from all walks of life. In 6 weeks' time, he produced a manuscript that was more than 500 pages long. It was published in February of the following year as *Pagan Spain: A Report of a Journey into the Past*.

Book critics found much to praise in Wright's fascinating descriptions of bullfights, markets, and Spanish terrain. His sympathetic portrayal of an oppressed people living under the iron rule of head of state Francisco Franco also won him much critical acclaim. Unfortunately, the book did not become a commercial success, and Wright needed the money from each new project to help make ends meet. Although his earlier works had sold well, they had not made him rich.

While preparing *Pagan Spain* for publication, Wright became involved in another project that he found extremely exciting: He helped the other members of the Présence Africaine organize the first conference ever held for black writers and artists from all over the world. The chief aim of the Conference

Editor and author W. E. B. Du Bois was America's leading black protest spokesman for more than half a century. His disillusionment with the U.S. government prompted State Department officials to restrict his traveling privileges, thereby preventing him from attending the 1956 Conference of Negro Writers and Artists that Wright helped coordinate in Paris.

of Negro Writers and Artists was for its participants to share their ideas for achieving racial harmony and to discuss international trends of thought. Wright was responsible for assembling the American delegates and managed to persuade the NAACP to finance the trip for those who were chosen to attend.

The four-day conference took place in Paris in September 1956. Among the American delegates were James Baldwin, Horace Mann Bond, James Ivy, and Mercer Cook. W. E. B. Du Bois, perhaps America's foremost black intellectual, had hoped to be a part of the American delegation, but the State Department denied him a passport because of his communist sympathies. Nevertheless, Du Bois sent a message to the participants, telling them, "Any Negro-American who travels abroad today must either not discuss race conditions in the United States or say the sort of thing which our State Department wishes the world to believe."

Wright was the last speaker to address the conference. His lecture on "Tradition and Industrialization" railed against black nationalism by calling for Western nations to industrialize Africa and help it grow. These remarks were later collected with three other essays ("Psychological Reactions of Oppressed People," "The Literature of the Negro in the United States," and "The Miracle of Nationalism in the African Gold Coast") and published in 1957 as *White Man, Listen!*

By then, Wright had already solidified his place as one of the best-known black writers in the world. Yet *Native Son*, *Black Boy*, and *Twelve Million Voices* were not earning him any money because they were no longer in print. As had happened to him on occasion in the past, he felt strapped financially. In addition, he and Ellen were having marital difficulties and were living apart.

The news from abroad was just as bad. He received word that his aunt Maggie, who had been living in

Jackson and had been taking care of his mother, had died of cancer. Furthermore, he was still being hounded for his political beliefs. Four U.S. government agencies—the FBI, the Central Intelligence Agency, the State Department, and the United States Information Service—kept him under surveillance. Magazine and newspaper articles included him in their repeated attacks on expatriate writers; among these articles was a piece by Ben Burns, who accused Wright of "poisoning European thinking about racial problems in America." Wright refused to travel to the United States and deal with these problems because he knew he would be asked to testify before a Senate subcommittee on his alleged un-American activities.

The turmoil continued after Wright's fourth novel, *The Long Dream*, was published in October 1958. The main character in the book is Fishbelly Tucker, a black Mississippi youth who struggles with the death of his father and learns about the horrors of racial prejudice. The reviews criticized Wright for writing about the American South as it had been more than 30 years ago, when he was a youth, and not as it was in the late 1950s, when the black civil rights movement, spearheaded by the Reverend Martin Luther King, Jr., was bringing about social change.

On the very day that Wright received the first negative reactions to *The Long Dream*, he received a telegram from his brother, Leon, informing him that their mother was seriously ill. She died a short time later, in January 1959. (Wright's father had died more than a decade earlier, shortly after their brief reunion in Mississippi.)

Wright's next projects were a sequel to *The Long Dream*, which is the still-to-be published "Island of Hallucinations," and a collection of short stories, *Eight Men*, which was published posthumously in 1961. The feverish pitch at which he worked on these

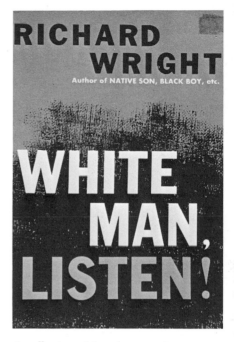

A collection of four lectures that Wright delivered in Europe, White Man, Listen! is chiefly a call for whites of the Western world to deal sympathetically with the Third World nations in Africa and Asia. "This useless struggle of having to prove one's humanity, which is a kind of supra racism, is the blight that the Western white man has cast upon the colored masses of Asia and Africa," he wrote.

During his lifetime, Wright published a short story collection, four novels, six books of nonfiction, and numerous articles, poems, reviews, and book introductions; three of his books were published posthumously. He became a writer, he explained, because, "I sensed that Negro life was a sprawling land of unconscious suffering and there were but few Negroes who knew the meaning of their lives, who could tell their stories."

books aggravated an intestinal virus he had picked up during his travels. By February 1960, he was ill almost constantly.

While convalescing in Paris, Wright concentrated on writing haikus, an unusual Japanese verse form. A haiku is a 3-line poem that contains 17 unrhymed syllables; in each line, there are 5, 7, and 5 syllables, respectively. All told, he produced more than 4,000 haikus. He attempted to put out a collection of these poems but was unable to find a publisher for them.

As 1960 wore on, Wright's health continued to deteriorate. On November 26, he began to experience dizzy spells and another recurrence of the intestinal virus. He made arrangements to check into the Eugene Gibez Clinic, a small hospital, for testing. Langston Hughes, who was visiting Wright in Paris, helped his longtime friend into a car that had arrived to take him to the clinic. Before riding away, Wright gave Hughes a manuscript to read, a play called *Daddy Goodness* that Wright had written four years earlier.

The doctors at the clinic tested Wright and found nothing seriously wrong with him. He simply needed rest, they told him. Wright telephoned his wife, who was working as a literary agent in England, and said the doctors had assured him he would be all right.

Wright died two days later, on November 28, 1960, at the age of 52. He had just been given an injection and was resting comfortably in his bed at the clinic when he suffered a fatal heart attack.

Wright often argued that black Americans "had never been allowed to catch the full spirit of Western civilization, that they somehow lived in it, but not of it." Yet his books did more to alter white society's perception of blacks and to raise the social conscience of his nation than the works of any other black author before him. No matter whether he was writing revolutionary poems, essays, travelogues, short stories, novels, or memoirs, he always acted as a spokesman for other native sons and daughters.

Even though Wright's best-known books were out of print at the time of his death, they did not go out of style. The powerful works of protest literature that influenced his contemporaries—including Chester Himes and J. Saunders Redding—went on to have a profound effect on succeeding generations of black authors, most notably among them Ralph Ellison, James Baldwin, and Imamu Amiri Baraka (the former LeRoi Jones). In fact, all of Wright's major writings, particularly *Native Son* and *Black Boy*, are in print once again, and his cry for racial equality can be heard in every one of them. ❧

APPENDIX: BOOKS BY RICHARD WRIGHT

1938   *Uncle Tom's Children: Four Novellas*
1940   *Native Son*
1941   *Twelve Million Black Voices: A Folk History of the Negro in the United States*
1945   *Black Boy: A Record of Childhood and Youth*
1953   *The Outsider*
1954   *Savage Holiday; Black Power: A Record of Reactions in a Land of Pathos*
1956   *The Color Curtain: A Report on the Bandung Conference; Pagan Spain*
1957   *White Man, Listen!*
1958   *The Long Dream*
1961   *Eight Men*
1963   *Lawd Today*
1977   *American Hunger*

CHRONOLOGY

1908   Born Richard Nathaniel Wright near Natchez, Mississippi, on September 4

1912   Moves to Memphis, Tennessee

1916   Begins formal education at the Howe Institute

1920   Enters the Jim Hill Public School in Jackson, Mississippi

1923   Enters the Smith-Robertson Public School

1924   Publishes his first short story, "The Voodoo of Hell's Half Acre"

1925   Graduates from Smith-Robertson as valedictorian; returns to Memphis

1927   Moves to Chicago

1932   Joins the Communist party

1934   Publishes his first protest poems

1937   Moves to New York; becomes editor of *New Challenge* and the *Daily Worker*

1938   Wins first prize in a literary contest; publishes his first book, *Uncle Tom's Children*

1939   Receives a Guggenheim Fellowship; marries Rose Dhimah Meadman

1940   Publishes his first novel, *Native Son*

1941   Marries Ellen Poplar; receives the Spingarn Medal; publishes his first nonfiction book, *Twelve Million Black Voices*

1942   First daughter, Julia, is born; Wright withdraws from the Communist party

1945   Publishes his autobiography, *Black Boy*

1947   Moves to Paris; joins the Présence Africaine

1949   Second daughter, Rachel, is born

1953   Wright visits Africa

1955   Attends the Bandung Conference in Indonesia

1960   Dies in Paris on November 28

FURTHER READING

Bakish, David. *Richard Wright.* New York: Ungar, 1973.

Bloom, Harold, ed. *Richard Wright.* New York: Chelsea House Publishers, 1987.

Brignano, Russell Carl. *Richard Wright: An Introduction to the Man and His Works.* Pittsburgh: University of Pittsburgh Press, 1970.

Fabre, Michel. *The Unfinished Quest of Richard Wright.* New York: Morrow, 1973.

Felgar, Robert. *Richard Wright.* Boston: Twayne Publishers, 1980.

Gayle, Addison, Jr. *Richard Wright: Ordeal of a Native Son.* New York: Doubleday, 1980.

Kinnamon, Kenneth, comp. *A Richard Wright Bibliography: Fifty Years of Criticism and Commentary.* Westport, CT: Greenwood Press, 1988.

Ray, David, and Robert M. Farnsworth, eds. *Richard Wright: Impressions and Perspectives.* Ann Arbor: University of Michigan Press, 1973.

Walker, Margaret. *Daemonic Genius.* New York: Warner Books, 1988.

Webb, Constance. *Richard Wright: A Biography.* New York: Putnam, 1968.

Williams, John A. *The Most Native of Sons.* New York: Doubleday, 1970.

Wright, Ellen, and Michel Fabre, eds. *Richard Wright Reader.* New York: Harper & Row, 1978.

INDEX

PICTURE CREDITS

JOAN URBAN holds a degree in English from Fordham University and has studied writing at New York University, City College of New York, and Columbia University. She has written for *Ingenue* and other publications and is currently director of library and academic marketing at a major publishing house in New York City.

NATHAN IRVIN HUGGINS is W.E.B. Du Bois Professor of History and Director of the W.E.B. Du Bois Institute for Afro-American Research at Harvard University. He previously taught at Columbia University. Professor Huggins is the author of numerous books, including *Black Odyssey: The Afro-American Ordeal in Slavery*, *The Harlem Renaissance*, and *Slave and Citizen: The Life of Frederick Douglass*.